Old Tiler Talks

By CARL H. CLAUDY

Author of "A Master's Wages," "The Old Past Master"
Editor CATHEDRAL CALENDAR
Associate Editor THE MASTER MASON

Published by
THE FELLOWSHIP FORUM
WASHINGTON, D. C.

*"Old Tiler Talks" are published weekly in The Fellowship Forum.
None of them, or any part of this book, can be reprinted
without permission*

To the Members of
The "Fourth Degree" of OLD HARMONY
(Lodge No. 17, F. A. A. M., District of Columbia)
If there is any wisdom in these pages, it is theirs

Foreword

MANY a learned man and Mason has written many a learned book and tome of the science, the art, the religion, the history, the symbolism of Freemasonry. This little book follows but very humbly in the footsteps they have left upon the Masonic sands, nor even pretends to imitate their greatness.

"Old Tiler Talks," which are published every week in *The Fellowship Forum,* are but a sincere attempt to put in every-day language some of the fundamentals of practical Masonry; to answer, in the words he understands, some of the questions that mythical person, "the average Mason," asks when he is yet but a Young Brother.

The author, himself a Masonic student in very elementary classes, bespeaks for the words of the Old Tiler but the same brotherly spirit in which he has tried to write them; he hopes for them, thus put forth in permanent form, only the welcome which the "common or garden" variety of Mason may have for sugar-coated pills of Masonic philosophy. He well knows that all that is here said, has been said before in many ways by most learned scholars; therefore he can and does claim no originality of thought. If there is anything in the homely words of the Old Tiler, to make any of the great truths of Masonry simpler to understand, and therefore easier to love, the author will feel more than repaid. Should the little book touch a responsive chord in the heart of some unknown brother, he will be a thousand times overpaid for its writing.

CARL H. CLAUDY.

CONTENTS

CONTENTS—Continued

On What Is Masonry

"WELL, I've been a Mason six months now and I ought to know something about Masonry. But there are more secrets in the fraternity I don't know than there are those I have been told!"

The New Brother was plainly puzzled. The Old Tiler laid down his sword, picked up a battered pipe and lit it, and settled back in his chair.

"Go ahead," he invited. "Get it out of your system."

"Well," went on the New Brother, "there's this matter of whether Masonry is a religion or a system of philosophy or just a childish getting together of men who like to play politics and wear titles. I have heard it called all three. And sometimes I think it's one and sometimes I think it's the other. What do you think?

"It isn't a childish getting together for the love of titles and honors," answered the Old Tiler. "If that was all there was to Masonry, man would soon invent a much better organization for the satisfaction of such purposes. In fact, he has invented better ones. There are several orders where elaborate titles, and a much more complicated political system hold sway. People who want to play politics and be called the Grand High Cockalorum of the Exalted Central Chamber of the Secret Sanctorum can join these. If Masonry were nothing but play, it wouldn't live, and living, grow.

"Masonry isn't a religion. A religion, as I see it, is a belief in a deity and a means of expressing worship of that deity. True, Masonry recognizes Deity, and proceeds only after asking Divine guidance. But it does not specify any particular deity. You can worship any God you please and be a Mason. That is not true of any religion. If you are a Buddhist, you worship Buddha. If a Christian, Christ is your Deity. If you are a Mohammedan you are a worshipper of Allah. In Masonry you will find Christian, Jew, Mohammedan and Buddhist side by side.

"Masonry has been called a system of philosophy, but that, to my mind is a confining definition. In fact, I don't think Masonry has ever been truly defined.

"Or God," put in the New Brother.

"Exactly. A very witty Frenchman, asked if he believed in God, once said, 'Before I answer you must tell me your definition of the word God. And when you tell me, I will answer you, no, because a God defined is a God limited, and a limited God is no God!' I think Masonry is something like that; it is brotherhood, unlimited, and when you limit it by defining it you have made it something it isn't."

"Deep stuff!" commented the New Brother.

"But Masonry is 'deep stuff,'" answered the Old Tiler.

"It's so deep no man has ever found the bottom. Perhaps that is its greatest charm; you can go as far as you like and still not see the limit. The fascination of astronomy is the limitlessness of the field. No telescope has so far seen to the edge of the universe. The fascination of Masonry is largely that it has no limit; the human heart has no limit in depth and of course that which appeals most to the human heart cannot have a limit.

"But that makes it so hard to understand!" sighed the New Brother.

"Well, isn't it the finer and the better for being difficult of comprehension?" asked the Old Tiler. "A few days ago I heard a very eminent divine and Mason make a wonderful and inspiring talk. I hear a lot of talks, you know, and nine-tenths of them are empty words with a pale tallow dip gleam of a faint idea somewhere in them. So when a real talker gets up and lets shine the full radiance of a whole idea on an audience, he is something to be remembered. So it was with this speaker. And in his speech he quoted a wonderful poem, by William Herbert Carruth. I asked him to send it to me, and he did; please note this busy man, president of a university and with a thousand things to do, didn't forget the request of a brother he never saw before!"

The Old Tiler put his hand in his pocket and took out a much-thumbed piece of paper. "Listen, you," he said, " 'till I read you something:

"A fire mist and a planet,
    A crystal and a cell,
A jellyfish and a saurian,
    And caves where cavemen dwell;
Then a sense of law and beauty
    And a face turned from the clod;
Some call it evolution
    And others call it God.

"A haze on the far horizon,
    The infinite, tender sky,
The ripe, rich tint of the cornfields,
    And the wild geese sailing high;
And all over upland and lowland
    The charm of the golden rod,
Some of us call it autumn,
    And others call it God.

"Like tides on a crescent sea-beach
    When the moon is new and thin,
Into our hearts high yearnings
    Come welling and surging in;
Come from the mystic ocean
    Whose rim no foot has trod;
Some of us call it longing
    And others call it God.

"A picket frozen on duty;
    A mother, starved for her brood;
Socrates drinking the hemlock,
    And Jesus on the rood;
And millions who, humble and nameless,
    The straight hard pathway plod;
Some call it consecration
    And others call it God."

The New Brother said nothing, held silent by
the beauty of the lines.

"I am no poet," said the Old Tiler, "and I
know this isn't very fitting, but I took out my
pencil and wrote something to go with those
lovely verses, just to read to brothers like you."
Shyly the Old Tiler continued:

"Many men, banded together
    Standing where Hiram stood;
Hand to back of the falling,
    Helping in brotherhood.
Wise man, doctor, lawyer,
    Poor man, man of the hod,
Many call it Masonry
    And others call it God."

"I don't think it makes much difference what
we call it, do you?" asked the New Brother.

Eight

On Sitting With the Sick

"YOU know I never did see much point in this joke about 'sitting up with the sick lodge members,'" said the Very New Brother to the Old Tiler, "but since I joined the lodge I begin to see light. I used to think people were making fun of what always seemed to me a very pretty idea; that a lodge member should go and sit up with a sick brother seemed a very real brotherhood. Now I find we don't do any such things, and of course I see the joke."

"Do you, now! How keen is your sense of humor?" answered the Old Tiler. "Who told you we didn't sit with our sick friends?"

"Why, no one. But if we did, I'd have heard of it, wouldn't I?"

"Depends on how long your ears are. The other day I went to buy a hat. The salesman showed me one and said it was fifteen dollars. I asked him where the holes were. He didn't know what holes I meant. So I explained I meant the holes for the ears of the jackass who would pay fifteen dollars for that hat. Now if you have ears long enough, maybe you could hear about our sitting up with our sick friends. But I presume, though you have ears long enough, you are hard of hearing.

"Listen, boy, till I tell you something. In small towns, in times of a few decades ago, nurses were few and far between. Men had to do their part and when a brother was sick, we often sat up with him, to cheer him, hand him water or medicine, doing what we could to alleviate his ills. In these modern days, with a doctor and a nurse on every street corner, there is less need for us to try to help our brethren in that way. But don't you get your head filled with the idea that we never do. Only last month the Master called for volunteers to sit up all night in a house where an old lady was dying. The brother, from that house, was out of town. The old lady had her daughter and her nurse, but her daughter was afraid to be in the house alone with death approaching. We had sixteen volunteers, and two every night for a week, did their part. All they did was sit there and read but who knows what comfort they were to that distracted daughter? The old lady finally died, not during the night, but in the day time. It looks, at first sight, as if what we did was wasted. But it wasn't. The old lady might have died in the night; our brethren were there to help the daughter if she did. The daughter knew her husband's brethren were within call; she slept, if she slept at all, secure in the protection Masonry threw about her.

"You say 'we don't sit up.' Don't confuse 'sitting up' with actually resting erect in a chair. Let me tell you, young man, that no brother of this or any other good lodge, can be reported sick and not receive a call from Master, Warden, chairman of sick committee, or some brother whose official as well as fraternal business it is to see that the sick are looked after. It makes no difference whether the sick one is wealthy or poor, high or low . . . we call to see what

Ten

we can do. Most members of the lodge are fairly prosperous citizens, able to look after themselves. But just because a man can pay for a doctor and a nurse and medical treatment, doesn't mean he isn't human enough to value the interest the lodge takes in him. The thought that the mighty brotherhood to which he belongs is anxious about him, in itself is a medicine. It acts as a tonic. We may never see the sick man; he may be too ill to admit us to his bedside, but they tell him about it, and it heartens him.

"The wealthiest member of this lodge was visited last year when he was sick. It happened that I was one of the visitors and that a chap whose business it was to run a street car was the other. The sick man is a banker, and president or director in half the companies in town. You'd think maybe he wouldn't have time for us? I tell you I never saw a man more pleased than Mr. Rich Man. He had us shown up to his room and he insisted we stay with him, and he talked lodge and asked questions and wanted information about the fellows just as if he was a poor man like the rest of us. He happens to be a real Mason as well as a wealthy man. After we left, he wrote a letter to the Master and said our visit had done him more good than his doctor, and wouldn't he please send us or some other brethren back?

"It isn't always what we do or say with the sick that helps. For instance, I called on a sick brother who was so ill he couldn't see me. But I saw his wife and his home and it was easy to see the brother needed help. But he was too proud to ask for it or his wife didn't know enough to ask the lodge for it. So I went back and reported and we had our own doctor and nurse on the job right away and fixed them up, and paid some bills and generally bossed the ranch until the brother got well. I am happy to say he has paid back every cent we spent on him, little by little, but he says he can never repay the brotherly kindness.

"Now, 'sitting up with a sick lodge member' may be a good alibi for the poker player; I don't know. I have read it in joke papers and heard it pulled on the stage. But I could never see much that was funny about it, because I know how well Masonry does care for her sick, and how much it means to an ill man to have his brother take an interest in him. If you know any sick, tell us. If you hear of any, tell us. And if—say, did you ever visit a sick brother?"

"I never had the chance," defended the Very New Brother.

"You mean you never made the chance for yourself!" countered the Old Tiler. "Now will you go to the sick committee and ask for duty or will I report your name for that duty to the Master? Or do you want to go on thinking it's a joke?"

"I got an earful, didn't I?" responded the New Member. "You tell me to whom to go and you bet I'll go.

"Humph," said the Old Tiler.

On Secrets of Free Masonry

"I THINK someone should speak to Brother Filmore," said the New Member, thoughtfully, sitting down beside the Old Tiler.

"Well, people do speak to him—I speak to him myself," countered the Old Tiler.

"But I mean, speak to him seriously."

"I speak to him seriously. I asked him to-night how his wife was," answered the Old Tiler.

"Oh, you know what I mean! I mean admonish him."

"About what?"

"About his carelessness of Masonic secrets. Here he is running the lantern and leaving the slides out in the boxes where any profane can see them. He takes them home sometimes and his children can get them and——"

"Well, I appoint you a committee of one to see that his children are all properly murdered. No child should look at a Masonic slide and live."

"Now you are kidding me."

"Boy, you are kidding yourself. What is there secret about a Masonic lantern slide? There is only one secret about them and thousands of Masons have tried to find it out and none ever have. But it is not to be revealed by looking at them.

"I don't understand——"

"No, but I'm telling you. There is nothing of the secrets of Freemasonry to be learned from a

Masonic lantern slide. They are sold in a hundred stores to any one who has the price. Filly can leave them all over the lot and do not a bit of harm. If there was anything secret about a lantern slide, making it would be against all Masonic obligations, or use!"

"But you just said there was a secret——"

"Sure, but not a Masonic secret. Generations of Masons have tried to find out who designed them, in order that they might slay him with ceremony and an axe. The harm done by leaving Masonic lantern slides where the profane may see them will come from the poor opinion the profane gets from the Masonic slide conception of charity and brotherly love and relief and truth. Those antedeluvian, prehistoric statues which represent Time counting the ringlets in the hair of the virgin are enough to give anyone with the slightest idea of art the notion that Masons are all cubists, which is all wrong. We are triangle-ists or rightanglists, maybe, but not cubists! Those illustrations of brotherly love, in which one fat man lays a ham-like arm lovingly about the bull-like neck of a misshapen Roman gladiator would scare any child who saw it into such fear of the fraternity he would probably weep every time Dad went to lodge . . . but as far as giving away any Masonic secrets is concerned—piffle!"

"Well, you evidently don't have the same reverence for the sacredness of Masonic secrets as I do."

"Whoa! Boy, you have things upside down. My reverence for real Masonic secrets is second to none. Your reverence is inclusive of everything; mine only for what experience has taught me is real. You wouldn't go home and tell your wife that a lodgeroom has a chair in the east, where the Master sits; that there is an altar in the center of the lodge; or that candidates take an obligation, would you?

"Certainly not!"

"Well, I would! The scrubwomen see the lodgeroom. If they can be permitted to view its sacred outlines, I see no reason why my wife shouldn't. In lodge entertainments we don't move the altar or the east—and women have entertained us after lodge was closed, more than once. Any catalogue of Masonic paraphernalia advertises hoodwinks, and ours are regularly sent to the laundry, anyhow!

"Now, lemme tell you something. The real secrets of Freemasonry are of value; they mean something—something for you and for me—which is not for the uninitiated. But the real secrets of Freemasonry are not in or upon lantern slides, the size of the room, the height of the ceiling or even the place where a Worshipful Master hangs his bat! Circumspection in speaking of the things of the lodge, as opposed to the spirit of a lodge, is necessary only that no false idea be given the outsider. For instance, if it were possbile to take a photograph of a class receiving the first degree, and to show it, the profane would laugh, utterly unappreciative of the symbolism of what they saw. But do you really think the value of Masonic secrets would be decreased by such an exhibition?

"Morgan, and a dozen other semi-insane men, have written what they were pleased to call 'exposes' of Masonry. Half true, half manufactured, no one was very much interested in them; on second-hand book stalls you can find them, pick them up for a few cents. You can find them in every Masonic library. I ask you, as a commonsense man and brother, if what they contained was really of harm to the fraternity, would the librarians not destroy them?

"Man, the secrets of Freemasonry are those things you carry in your heart; not the things you see with your eyes or can touch with your fingers. There is nothing secret about an organ, or the music books the choir uses, or the gavel the Master holds in his hand, nor yet the books the Secretary uses to record who hasn't paid his dues. The shape and form and furniture of a lodge is not a secret, nor is the time of meeting or the name of the Chaplain. The lantern slide conceals no secret worth knowing, nor does the chart to which the lecturer points nor even the carpet laid down in the second degree. These are all but means of putting a picture in your mind and it is that picture, and its meaning, which must be sacredly kept, not the means which put it there.

"Then you don't think someone ought to speak to Brother Filmore seriously!"

"No, but there was a brother in this lodge who had to be spoken to seriously. I did it."

"Why, who was it?" asked the New Brother anxiously.

"You," said the Old Tiler.

On Knowing Names

"I'VE been watching you for half an hour and you haven't missed calling a single brother by his name," said the New Brother to the Old Tiler. "How do you do it?"

"How do I remember names? Why, that's my business. As tiler, I am supposed to know all the brethren of this lodge. I get paid for being a tiler. If I didn't know my job I would certainly be taking money under false pretenses."

"I don't mean so much how do you remember names," answered the New Brother, "as how did you learn them? I have been a member of this lodge for nearly a year. And I guess I must know all of a dozen men by name. How do you do it?"

"How do you not do it?" countered the Old Tiler. "Don't you ever know any one by name in any organization you belong to?"

"Well, er—I——"

"I visited in one lodge once," interrupted the Old Tiler, "where they used the scheme which is a part of Rotary, Kiwanis, Lion, Civitan, and Optimists clubs. The Master started a sort of automatic roll call, in which each brother in turn stood up, gave his name and address and business and sat down again. It smacked a little of the commercial to me; the business giving didn't sit very well. To hear a chap get up and say, 'My name is Bill Jones, agent for the Speedemup car, in business at 1576 Main Street,' may be very informing to the brother who doesn't know it, but it seems a little like advertising. However, I presume the scheme worked; everyone in that lodge got to know everyone else by name in time.

"In another lodge I know of, every brother wears a name plate. It is a big, round, celluloid affair, and has his name printed on it in big letters. The tiler, poor chap, has charge of a big rack and is supposed to see that every brother entering the room has his button on and that none go away wearing it when the lodge is over. This, too, is a scheme which works; you can go up to a brother and read his name and call him by it, and probably remember it next time.

"But none of these ideas ever seem so good to me as the thing they are supposed to be short cuts to. Ready-made brotherhood is the dream of the professional Mason; ready-made acquaintance is the thing he strives for with his announcements and his celluloid buttons.

"As a matter of fact, I don't regard the use of a name as at all essential. It is pleasant to be called by name and nice to be able to remember names. But a name, after all, is an artificial distinction, conferred on us by our parents, a minister and society, as a matter of convenience. Someone has said that a rose smells just as sweet if you call it a sunflower, and a man is just the same if you call him Jim or Jones. Not very long ago a man came up to me on the street and said, 'I don't know your name but I know you are tiler of my lodge. My uncle down in the country has just sent me a crate of strawberries. I can't use 'em all and I'd like to have you have some. Will you write your name and address on a card so I can send them?'

"Now, if he had known my name he could have sent them without asking for the card. But would they have tasted any better? I had a little warm feeling at my heart; my brother had remembered my face and who I was, and wanted me to share in his good luck; that he didn't know my name didn't seem to matter to me. He knew me.

"It's a fine and friendly thing, calling a man by his name. We are all more or less egocentric. (I heard Doc Palmer use that word and he tells me it means that we revolve about ourselves.) And when people remember our names we think we must have made an impression on them, which tickles our vanity. There are half a dozen members in this lodge who come only once a year. I always call them by name and they always swell up like a poisoned pup. But they wouldn't if they knew my system. One of them has unusually prominent ears; so has a jackass. A jackass eats thistles. This man's name is Nettleton. Another chap has a nose that looks as if it grew on a Brobdingnagian face. His name is Beekman. Now it's no trick to remember them, but I don't remember them because of any impression they have made on me except a physical one of ugliness. I remember your name as an earnest young brother trying to learn. I remember the past masters by remembering their services. I know

Nineteen

John and Jim and George and Elly and Harry
and Joe and Frank and the rest because I know
the men, know what they do, how they do it, what
they stand for in the lodge and in Masonry; in
other words, it's the brother I know first, and in
my mind I tack a name to him. Merely to remember a name, and tack a face to it is the trick
accomplished by the celluloid button, the automatic roll call, in fact, by all schemes to get men
to know each other by name with the idea that
the name and not the man and his personality is
the important thing.

"You tell me you have been here nearly a year
and know a dozen men by name. If you know a
hundred by sight so you can speak to them when
you see them, you have done something much
more important than merely filling your memory
with names. But if you know only your dozen
by sight and name, and no others either by sight
or name, then I say there is something the matter
with the way you sit in lodge, something the matter with your idea of fellowship.

"A lodge is a place where brothers can learn to
know each other; if they can learn each other's
names in the process, well and good; indeed, fine
and dandy. But if they can learn to know each
other as men, as brothers, as friendly faces, as
real human beings, then it does not make much
difference in the long run whether they have good
or poor memories for names.

"Our Master to-day is a fine man, a lovable
man. Every dog he meets on the street wags his
tail and speaks to him; and he speaks to them all.
But I doubt if he knows their names. He has a
poor memory for names, yet he never forgets a

Twenty

face. I know names and faces because it's my job, but I'd make a poor Master. Get me, boy?"

"I get you but I'm not so sure about your being a poor Master!"

"Well, I am. Don't confuse a good Mason, a good man and a good Master. I try to be the first, anyhow."

On Being Asked to Join

"I THINK it's an outrage," announced the New Brother with great emphasis, and talking at, if not to, the Old Tiler.

"Sure it is," answered the Old Tiler.

"Well, why don't you have it stopped, then?"

"I dunno; what is it?"

"Why, you just agreed with me it was an outrage. And now you don't know what it is."

"No more I do. But I am wise enough to agree with brethren out of temper—then they don't get out of temper with me. So suppose you tell me what it is that is an outrage?"

"Why, the way all these fellows try to get me to join things. Ever since I was raised they have been after me. Jones wants me to join his Chapter and Smith says as soon as I do that I must come in his Council, and Robinson wants me in his Commandery and Jackson says I mustn't think of going York but must go Scottish Rite, and Brown is already talking of what he is going to have done to me when he gets me to join the Shrine, and Peters wants me to become a Veiled Prophet and Lem says I mustn't forget the Tall Cedars, and then there's old Jerry tells me he'll never let up on me until I join the Eastern Star . . . it makes me ill."

"You sure do get sick easy," answered the Old Tiler. "But I'll attend to it. Tomorrow I will see to it that not less than ten brethren come to you and tell you you are not good enough for the Chapter, not wise enough to join the Council, not brainy enough for the Rite, not sincere enough for the Commandery, not a good enough sport to stand the Grotto, Tall Cedars or Shrine initiation and not decent enough to join the woman's organization. That'll fix it all right and you can be well again."

"Here, wait a mintute. What you mean, I am not decent enough for the women or good enough sport to stand the Shrine! I'll have you know I'm perfectly decent and as good a sport as——"

"Gently, gently; I did not say you were not—I said I'd arrange with a lot of brethren to tell you you were not."

"But why?"

"Well, you get peeved and say it's an outrage when they tell you the other thing—I thought that was what you wanted."

"I don't understand you. Our wires are crossed somewhere!"

"No, it is you who are cross and therefore not able to see straight," snapped the Old Tiler. "You say it's an outrage that many brethren invite you to join with them. What is there outrageous about it? The fellow who wants to have you in his Chapter sees in you good material out of which to make a Companion. The Knight who wants you in his Commandery thinks you will grace its uniform, live up to its high standards, conform to its usages. The brother who would like to have you in the Scottish Rite thinks you have brains enough to appreciate the erudite and philosophic degrees there conferred and believes that Albert Pike had such as you in mind when he wrote 'Morals and Dogma.' The Noble or the Veiled Prophet who asks you to come with him thinks you are a good sport, able to be the butt of a joke for a while that others may laugh, and that you may, in turn, enjoy the antics of others. They all take you for a regular fellow. When you are asked to join the Eastern Star a great compliment is paid you—you are selected as a Mason who is fit to associate with fine women in a woman's organization; you are accepted as a gentleman as well as a Mason; a man women will be proud to know. And all you can find to say about it is 'it's an outrage.' "

"Well, of course, I never looked at it just that way. I have learned that Masons do not ask others to join with Masons in Masonry and I suppose I thought—I felt——"

"As I have told you before, you didn't really think; you just thought you thought." The Old Tiler was smiling now. "But think again. There is every reason why Masonry should not ask the profane to be of it. Masonry is bigger than any man. It never seeks; it should always be sought. But once a Mason, the case is different. The Blue Lodge has investigated you. You have been tried and found not wanting by your fellows, otherwise they wouldn't admit you to the lodge. Why should not your brother ask you to join another organization in which he is interested and which he thinks will interest you?"

"Well, but——"

"But nothing! There is no 'but' which fits the case. There are many Masonic organizations, each filling its place. Chapter, Council, and Commandery, extend the Blue Lodge story; the Scottish Rite also tells it to the end and far beyond;

Shrine, Grotto and Tall Cedars are happy places where good Masons play. The Eastern Star has its ends in sisterhood, in charity, benevolence, kindness, the softer, prettier, gentler side of life. None duplicate; all have work to do. The better the workers, the better done is the work. Why is it an outrage that they pay you the deep and lasting compliment of asking you to join with them?"

"Well, of course, I haven't the time; I don't know if I could afford it."

"Ah, well, that is another story altogether. All these organizations cannot make you more a Mason than you are now, but they can make you a better one. But as to whether you have the time or the small means needed, that is your own affair. It would indeed be an outrage if I or anyone questioned you about that. But they pay you also the compliment, these brethren who ask you to join with them, of thinking you have leisure enough to be a better Mason and means enough to indulge that laudable ambition."

"Oh, of course, you are right and I am wrong, as usual. I guess I'm a——"

"A Mason," suggested the Old Tiler, gently.

"Exactly; and a prospective Companion, Knight or whatever it is they will call me when I join the Scottish Rite and the Shrine and the rest!"

On Poor Fish!

"IF it wasn't that I loved the old lodge so much I'd demit and go to a live one."

The Senior Member spoke disgustedly to the New Brother. The Old Tiler laid down his sword, hitched up his chair and snorted.

"S'matter with the old lodge now?" he asked belligerently.

"Oh, same old thing. Same old gang. No possible chance of doing anything different than we ever did. No pep. No costumes. No new expenditure for anything. We have died on the vine and don't know it!"

"Some one step on a resolution you offered?"

"Didn't offer any. Knew better. No use asking that bunch to do anything."

"Listen, brother, till I give you some advice. Go to the aquarium and consider the fishes."

"Huh!"

"I said it. Consider the fishes—the poor fishes. I did. I talked to the master of the aquarium, too. I asked him how he kept a bass in a glass pot full of water and small minnows, and what kept the bass from eating up his companions. He told me he had trained the bass not to eat minnows. When I asked him how the Sam Hill he could do that, he told me he put a plate glass partition in an aquarium, with the minnows on one side and the bass on the other. The bass, he said, made a nose dive after a mouthful of minnows and got a noseful of invisible plate glass. That rather gave him a pause for a moment but he soon returned. For three days at intervals that determined bass tried to dive through the glass he couldn't see. After the third day his nose was so sore he gave up. Decided, probably, that the minnows were ghost minnows and couldn't be eaten and so he gave up trying. He has lived with them a year since and never tried to eat one, even when it rubs against his nose.

"Now, brother, you go consider the poor fish. He doesn't try anything because once he did and got a sore nose. You think there is a lot the matter with the old lodge because it won't spend money for costumes or stage an entertainment or buy a new temple or something. You are convinced it has died on the vine, because it hasn't done anything progressive for some time. Everyone in that room there talks the same way. They all know everyone wants to do something, but once, a few years ago, there was a crowd of stand-patters in the saddle and they put a plate glass down between the membership and any minnows of progress. The plate glass is gone long ago; the little ring of stand-patters is a ring no more. But you and all the rest like you are afraid to offer any constructive program because you think that plate glass is still there.

"As between the bass and you and those like you, I don't think there's much difference in wealth."

"Wealth; I don't just get you!"

"I said wealth. You are both poor fish."

"That's handing it out pretty straight," said the New Brother. "Now tell me, Mr. Tiler, why this old and successful lodge should spend any money for anything except necessities and charity? It is a good lodge, a flourishing lodge, an old lodge."

"Got any loose change in your pocket?" asked the Old Tiler.

"Sure, handful," said the New Brother, pulling it out.

"Fine," said the Old Tiler. "Now you lay it all down on that chair except a dime. Take up a dime, hold it in front of one eye and close the other eye. What do you see?"

"Why, I see a dime, of course!" was the surprised answer.

"Exactly. You see a dime. You don't see the $1.87 on the chair. You got a dime so close to your face you can't see $1 a foot away. That's what's the matter with people who don't want to spend lodge money for anything they don't have to. They see the treasury getting full to bursting and investments piling up and they take a dime out of their pocket and try to look through it. They are so scared to spend a dollar they don't dare even read the treasurer's report aloud for fear some one will steal it!

"Well, it's a fine old lodge, running on its reputation. It used to spend money, and spend it wisely. Everything we needed we had. We had jamborees and smokers and entertainments; we had picnics and outings; we had educational lectures and a library; we had constructive work done all the time on new brethren and candidates. We spent what we took in and made better and happier Masons by so doing. Then, gradually we got to looking at the thin dimes so hard we couldn't see the dollars of advertising, of success, of progress, of reputation, we had made for ourselves. The dimes in the treasury hid the dollars of Masonic success from our eyes. So we stopped spending. Now we got a lot of money and a reputation with our own members of having died on the vine. What shall it profit a lodge if it lay up large numbers of dollars in the treasury, and lose its hold on its members? Where is the profit of penuriousness and lack of progress, even if we have money? What good is money? None, unless you spend it. A million dollars at the North Pole isn't as valuable as one fur coat. All the money in the world on a desert island wouldn't do a soul any good. You've got to spend money to get the good of it. You got to spend money to make money. And you got to spend money to keep your lodge alive and make your members better members and your Masons better Masons."

"I never thought of it just that way before," hesitated the New Brother.

"No, I know you didn't. I think I'll start a public acquarium."

"What for?" the New Brother was unwise enough to ask.

"For poor fish, of course," snapped the Old Tiler. "I've got two right here now to start with."

"Come on in that lodge room with me," said the New Brother firmly to the Old Tiler. "No Old Tiler can call me a poor fish and get away with it."

"Why, what are you going to do?" asked the Senior Member.

"Going to offer a resolution to spend $1,000 in the next six months in educational work among our own members, and you are going to second it."

"There goes the start of a perfectly good aquarium," sighed the Old Tiler as he let him in. But he smiled as he said it.

On Finding Things Out

"I'M sore," announced the New Brother to the Old Tiler.

"Where?" demanded the Old Tiler. "I'm no doctor, if it's your teeth or your back."

"It isn't. It's my feelings."

"Oh, well, that's different. As a soother of sore Masonic feelings I am the best little doctor in captivity!" smiled the Old Tiler. "Pull out your symptoms and let's look at them."

"Well, it's being jumped on, if you must know," began the New Brother. "I asked a friend of mine to give me his petition to the lodge and Brother Smith heard it and took me aside and walked all over me. How was I to know we didn't go around asking for petitions? A few days ago a fellow I know, at lunch, made a lot of slighting remarks about Masonry and I defended it and a Brother who was present took me to task afterwards and told me I shouldn't discuss Masonry with the profane. How was I to know it wasn't done in the best Masonic circles? Just this evening I answered the telephone and a feminine voice asked for Brother Jones and I said he wasn't here, and the Master walked up and down my spine for giving out any information as to who was and who wasn't present. How was I to know that was a secret?"

"Well, how do you usually find things out?" asked the Old Tiler.

"But I think I ought to be told these things. I think I should be instructed, told what to do and what not to do. I think——"

"I don't think you think," interrupted the Old Tiler. "I think you think you think but you don't. You just react. Now you listen to me and answer a few questions, like a good patient, and I'll cure your pimpled feelings, relieve the congestion in your inflamed emotions and reduce the swelling in your cranium and you'll feel a lot better.

"In the first place, what's your business?"

"Why, I am in the hardware business—I own the store at the corner of Main and Oak Streets —what's that got to do with it?"

"When you went into the hardware business, did you know all there was to know about it?"

"I'll say I didn't and don't now. But what——"

"I'm doing the question asking!" snapped the Old Tiler. "Did all the other hardware dealers of this town flock around you and give you good advice? Did they all surround you day and night with counsel and assistance? Or did they let you paddle your own canoe?"

"Just that. I learned what I know by asking questions and reading, by listening to others who knew the game, by——"

"Exactly. You hung up a sign and launched out for yourself, and they accepted you at your own value—as a competitor, a man, a business agent, able to fight your own battles. That's what we do in the lodge. We make you a Master Mason. We give you instruction in Masonry. We make you one of us. Then we turn you loose and expect you to act as if you were a man and a Mason, not a school child. If we spent all our time telling every new brother all we know, we'd have no time to practice brotherhood. We expect you to open not only your ears but your mouth. There are seventy-six men in that lodge to-night, any one of whom will answer any question you ask, and if they don't know the answer they will find some one who does. But to expect the seventy-six to come and force information on you is to be unreasonable. They don't know what you know; they have the natural human reluctance to seem to put themselves in the position of teacher, when they don't know if you want to learn or what you want to learn. Just ask a question and you'll hear something. Stick around with your mouth shut and you won't.

"The fraternity has certain customs and usages. Those who denounce it in public can do it no harm, but defense can harm it. If a man gets up in public and says he thinks the public school is useless, the church a bad influence, and the government a failure, banks a hindrance to business and the automobile a blot on civilization, do you think you have to defend the school, the church, the government, the bank, the automobile? Every thinking human being knows the public school has made this country what it is, that the church makes men and women better, that this is the best of all governments and that the automobile is the greatest of time savers. These things are self-evident. The man who denies them makes himself ridiculous, not the thing he criticizes. So with criticism of Masonry —it hurts the man who utters the criticism, not the thing criticized. To defend the institution in public is to make yourself of the same class as the man who criticises."

"All that is true. I admit it, but I didn't know it."

"No, and you didn't know you were not supposed to say Brother Jones wasn't here when he was, or wasn't here. That's his business. But I'm telling you. And I'm telling you because you asked me. I thought you knew all this. How was I to know you didn't? You never told me you didn't."

"Well, er—I thought—I mean——"

"You thought you thought but you thought wrong!" smiled the Old Tiler. "Son, just remember this; don't do anything, don't say anything, don't even think about Masonry while you are new until you have asked. We are old, old; we have customs and usages, ideas, ways of doing, even ways of thinking, which have grown up through the years with us. You will learn them gradually as you attend lodge and as you talk with well-informed Masons. Don't be afraid to open your mouth in lodge. No one will laugh at you, all will help. But don't ask questions outside the lodge and don't talk outside the lodge until you know what you are talking about."

"I know one place outside the lodge where I can, do and shall talk!" defended the New Brother.

"In spite of what I say?" demanded the Old Tiler somewhat tartly.

"Yep, in spite of what you say. And that place is right here in the ante-room," smiled the New Brother. "And thank you."

"Umph!" grunted the Old Tiler.

On Belief In God

"YOU know my old friend Jimmy, don't you? Well, he asked me to put his petition in the lodge, and I don't know what to do."

"Why not? Good man, isn't he?"

"Best ever. It isn't that. But Jimmy has said a lot of times he doesn't know what he believes. I don't think he is an atheist, but he certainly has some leaning towards being an agnostic. And I don't know whether he can answer the question about believing in God honestly."

"Well, what's that to you?"

"Why, I don't want to put a man's petition into lodge if I think he's going to lie about his beliefs."

"Certainly not; but is Jimmy a liar?"

"No, but——"

"No buts. He is a liar or he isn't. If you know him for a truthful, honest man, you haven't any business wondering in advance about how he is going to answer the question as to his belief in Deity. You have just as much right, and no more, to question his honesty before he answers the question as to whether he knows any physical, legal or moral reason why he should not become a Freemason. If you doubt that he would tell the truth about one question you must doubt that he would tell the truth about all the questions."

"Oh, but I know Jimmy wouldn't lie about those things——"

"Then why should he lie about the other?"

Thirty-five

"Because of things he has said to me."

"Then put a petition in front of him, point that question out to him, and tell him you want it answered first. If he answers it as he should, you sign his petition and forget your questions. A man's belief in his God is his private, personal affair. If he is publicly an atheist, he won't dare become a believer for lodge purposes only. If he is an atheist and honest, he won't sign that petition himself, let alone ask you to sign it."

"But, listen. You haven't got my drift yet. What I want to know is, isn't there some way I can help him get a grip on his wandering ideas?"

"You are asking me how to convince a man that there is a Grand Architect of the Universe? Well, you asked the right man. I have had the faith of my mother all my life, but I once read that a famous astronomer said, 'no man can look through a telescope and not believe in God.' So I made it my business to find out if that was true. I got myself a permit to look at the wonderful machine which is the solar system through a great telescope. And, boy, I'm here to tell you that the astronomer who said that was right."

"Tell me about it?"

"I'm telling. I went out to the observatory at nine o'clock. The observatory is out in the country, of course, where no city lights interfere with the seeing. The astronomer invited me into the dome. I entered a place so dimly lit it was like a church—lofty, vaulted dome, dim to black overhead, and one long dark blue slit which showed stars—the cut in the dome through which the telescope points. I asked my friend the astronomer why he had it so dark. He told me that if they made it light inside my eyes wouldn't be open enough to see the faintly lit wonders of the telescope. Then he asked me what I wanted to see and I told him I didn't care—I was looking for wonders."

"Well, he said 'Saturn,' and turned to a book and looked up some figures. Then he touched some buttons and the huge engine which was the telescope commenced very slowly to turn. It revolved and turned over. A thing like a banshee wailed off to one side—that was an electric motor turning the huge iron dome. Then the professor fooled around with some levers and buttons and finally the floor on which I stood rose up with me till I could get my eye to the telescope.

"I looked. There was a great ball like fire, with rings around it. The astronomer had found it out of all the countless stars in heaven by looking for some figures in a book, and setting the telescope to those figures.

" 'How did you know where to look?' I asked him.

" 'We know just where every planet is now and just where it will be any moment at any time in the future. They move according to law—simple, unvarying and absolute,' he answered.

"Well, that was what I came to see. I saw a lot of other marvels—a double-double star, a system of four suns revolving in pairs and each pair about the other; a nebula, which some day may be a solar system; a comet, strange wanderer in space—and always there was first the book, then the moving telescope which always pointed as if by magic to the thing the astronomer wanted to find. That was enough for me, I say—the fact that all that mighty heavens moved and was according to law—that we, down here, little insects of people, had found out the law and were able to point our space-penetrating engine where the thing we wanted to see was, without ever a mistake.

"But I don't see—you mean——"

"I mean that everything up there is planned. Planets move according to a plan. The comets move according to a plan. We don't know what the end of the plan may be, but we know the movements. We never find them different from what our explorations and calculations say they will be. If they move according to plan, some one must have made the plan. A plan without a planner is as unthinkable as a sight without eyes, a sound without ears, light without a source.

"Take your friend to an observatory. Let him see for himself what I have seen—let him realize as I have realized that the mightiest machine in our vision and knowledge is as invariable as eternity; let him see that it is a plan and that he cannot, if he have a brain, deny the Planner. He may call the Planner what he will, God or Great First Cause, or Absolute Eternity or just Deity— we do not ask him to define God when he expresses a belief in Him."

"I'll do it. And say, Old Tiler, why don't you get in line and be a Master? You ought to——"

"Oh, no. Do much more good out here—educating youngsters who don't know anything!" grinned the Old Tiler.

On Getting Something Out of Lodge

"ELL, brother, how do you like it now you've been a member six months?" asked the Old Tiler.

"Well, I am getting discouraged," was the dejected answer.

"Tell me about it," said the Old Tiler, leaning his sword up against the wall and making himself comfortable in his chair.

"Well, I guess maybe I expect too much. My dad was a Mason and he always thought a lot of it—he was a Past Master and a trustee and a representative to several bodies with which his lodge had affiliations. He talked a good deal about the friends one made in lodge and how valuable they are and the spirit of brotherhood I'd find there, and how Masons all helped each other. And I haven't found any of that. I come to the meetings and listen to the degrees, of course, and I find them beautiful. But it's all talk so far as I am concerned. I don't know any one in lodge, and I am not really a part of it—I just play audience."

"Humph," grunted the Old Tiler. "You remind me of a story. A chap came to a wise man and said, 'Tell me what's the matter with me. I'm not popular. People don't like me. They leave when I come around. I like people; I don't like to be unpopular. What's the matter with me?'

"The wise man looked his inquirer over and then said, 'What do you do when you are alone?'

" 'I don't do anything when I am alone,' was the answer, 'because I am never alone. I hate to be alone. It bores me. I bore myself. I have to be with people to be happy.'

"The wise man smiled and answered, 'How do you expect not to bore other people if you bore yourself? The man who has no resources to interest himself, cannot expect to interest others. Go, read, think, reflect, get an idea, a personality, a smile, a story, an accomplishment—learn something, do something, be something, amuse yourself, please yourself, interest yourself, and you can please, interest and amuse others!' "

"I see," said the Discouraged Brother. "You mean I find nothing of brotherhood in lodge because I bring no brotherhood to it?"

"You hit it the first shot!" exclaimed the Old Tiler. "Now listen while I tell you something. Masonry offers a whole treasure house for any and all of her children who take it. But it has to be taken. She doesn't take and stuff her treasures down your throat. Your father was a Past Master. That means he gave years of service to the lodge. He was a trustee—that means he was well known and liked, well trusted. Men do not get well known, well liked and well trusted by sitting in a corner listening. They must get up and talk, get out and work, do something, serve their fellows, to be known and liked. Your father brought rich treasures of service, interest, ability to his lodge. His lodge gave him back of its best—honor, responsibility, respect, love. You

Forty

come and sit on the benches and listen—but that's all. We made you a Master Mason but only you yourself can make you a good one. We give you privileges—only you can enjoy them. We give you opportunities—but only you can use them. We did all we could for you, and now we wait for you to prove yourself.

"Many a man comes into the lodge expecting it to act as a special reception committee, crowding around him at every meeting, saying how glad it is to have him there. Many a man is disappointed. You have our undivided attention as a candidate, as an Initiate, as a Fellowcraft, and while we make you a Master Mason. Now it's your turn. We are through with your candidacy —you are now a part of the lodge. For every privilege you have there is a duty attached. When you perform those duties, you will find other privileges awaiting you. If you never perform them, you will never get any further. It is only fair that the responsibility we assumed in putting the seal of our approval upon you as a man worthy to be a Master Mason and sit with us should be shared by you. You have now the responsibility of being a good Mason and a good lodge member. There are good Masons who are poor lodge members, but they are not the beloved ones. The beloved lodge member, like your father, finds much to do, much to labor, much to serve, and takes his pay in the spirit of fraternity, in the love and admiration of other men, in the satisfaction which comes from playing his part."

"But what can I do—what is my first step?"

"You want to make friends in the lodge?"

"I surely do!"

"Then go and be a friend. I am told that the Master read out to-night that Brother Robinson is ill. Go and see him. I have heard that old Willis is back to work, been sick a year. Call him up and tell him you are glad. Hungerford just got back from the West. He is out of a job and wants help. Ask him to come and see you and talk to him. Maybe you can help him, maybe you can't. But if a brother takes an interest in him, he will be heartened and given courage. Go to the Master and ask him for a job—tell him you want to serve. He'll use you, never fear. We have a sister lodge coming to visit us next month —you have a car, offer it to the chairman of the entertainment committee. Bob always has trouble getting enough personal news of the membership to fill his personal column in the paper; scout around a little and learn a few things and tell him about them. I understand you play the piano. Go talk to the choirmaster—offer your help when he needs some one to take the organist's place some night. Man, there are one thousand and one ways a chap can make himself known and liked in a lodge. All you have to do is look for them."

"I see——"

"Not yet, you don't see. But you soon will. And this is what you will see when your eyes are opened. A lodge is a mirror—when you look for yourself in it you will see just what you are. And if the reflection is dejection, dissatisfaction, un-happiness, it is because those are the things you are. When you look in the lodge and find yourself happy, busy, well liked, giving service and taking joy in service and brotherhood as a return, you will know that you are a real Mason, a real lodge member, a real son to a father who learned that the real secret of Masonic joy is to give, that it may be given back to you."

"You are right. Say, don't you want to get a smoke? I'll stay on the door until you come back!"

On a Country Lodge

"IT was the funniest thing I ever saw!"'

"What was?" asked the Old Tiler of the New Brother.

"Why, that lodge meeting I attended in Hicksville. Listen, and I'll tell you!"

"I'm listening. Any one who can find anything funny in a lodge meeting deserves to be listened to!" answered the Old Tiler, "Shoot the tale."

"You'd have died laughing!" began the New Brother. "First place, the lodge room was funny! Lodge rooms ought to have leather-covered furniture and electric light, a handsome painting in the east, an organ—be dignified, like ours. This lodge room was over the post office. There were two stoves in it—just think of it! And every now and then the Junior Deacon had to go and put coal on! The lesser lights were three kerosene lamps, and the altar looked like an overgrown soap box! The benches were not benches at all, just chairs, and they didn't have any lantern or slides—just an old chart to point things out on in the lecture.

"But it wasn't so much the room, it was the way they did their work. Honestly, you'd have thought they were legislating for a world, not just having a business meeting. Such preciseness, such slow walking, such making every move and sign as if they were drilled for a drill team. There wasn't a smile cracked the whole evening and even when at refreshment, there wasn't any

talking or laughing. Oh, it was rich. I'm glad
I attend a lodge where people are human.!"

"Yes," answered the Old Tiler, "I expect it
is."

"Expect what is?"

"Expect it is impossible for a New Brother to
understand the work of a country lodge,"
answered the Old Tiler. "Now you listen till I
tell you that what you saw wasn't funny. It is
you who are funny."

"Me funny? Why, what do you——"

"I said for you to listen!" sternly cut in the
Old Tiler. "I have never been to Hicksville and
I don't know that lodge, but I have visited in
many country lodges and your description of
them is accurate. But your interpretation of
what you describe is damnable!

"Masonry is in itself beautiful, truthful, phil-
osophical, strives to draw men closer to God, to
make them love their fellows, to be better men.
Is there anything funny in that? Of course not.
The more regard men have for the outward symbols of anything, the more apt they are to have
regard for what is within. A man who won't
clean his face and hands won't have a clean heart
and mind. A man who is slovenly and careless
in dress is apt to be careless and slovenly in his
heart. A lodge which reveres the work probably
reveres the meaning behind the work.

"You criticise the Hicksville lodge because it
is too precise. Would that our own was more so!
The officers who have so deep a regard for appearances can only have learned that deep regard
through a thoughtful and reverent appreciation
of what the appearances stand for.

"As for the externals, have you not been taught that it is not the externals but the internals which mark the man and Mason? What possible difference can it make whether a lodge seats its membership on leather benches or chairs, or the floor, or doesn't seat them at all? Our ancient brethren, so we are taught, met on hills and in valleys. Think you that they sat upon leather benches, or the grass?

"It's nice to have a fine hall to meet in. It's a joy to have a fine organ and electric lights and a stereopticon to show handsome slides of the degrees. But all of these are merely easy and pleasant ways of teaching the Masonic lesson. Doubtless Lincoln would have enjoyed electric lights to study by, instead of firelight. Doubtless he would have learned a little more in the same time had he had more books and better facilities. But he learned enough, didn't he, to make him live forever?

"We teach in a handsome hall, with beautiful accessories. If we teach as well, as truly and as thoroughly as the poor country lodge with its chairs for benches, its kerosene lamps for lesser lights, its harmonium for organ, its chart for lantern slides, we can congratulate ourselves. And while we look at the little lodge with its humble equipment, let us thank the Great Architect, that there is in existence so grand a system of philosophy, with so universal an appeal, as to make men content to study it and so to practice it, regardless of external conditions.

"I do not know Hicksville Lodge. But it would be at least an even bet that they saved up enough money to get better lodge furniture and then spent it to send some sick brother South or West, or to provide an education for the orphan children of some brother who couldn't do it for his children. In a country lodge you will get a sandwich and a cup of coffee after the meeting, in place of the elaborate banquet you may eat in the city; in the country lodge you will find few dress suits and not often a fine orator, but you will also find a Masonic spirit, a willingness to suffer for the good of a brother, a feeling of genuine brotherly regard, which is all too often absent in the larger, richer, city lodge.

"No, my brother, I would find nothing 'funny' in the dignity and the seriousness your country brethren have. I would find nothing of humor in the poverty, nor anything but Masonic service in the Junior Deacon putting coal on the fire. Would that we had a few brethren as serious, to put coal upon our Masonic fires, to warm us all."

"I think you've put coals of fire on my head!" answered the New Brother; "I deserved a kicking and got off with a lecture. I'm going back to Hicksville lodge next week and tell them what they taught me through you."

"Uh-huh," grunted the Old Tiler, but his eyes smiled.

On Secrecy of Ballot

"WELL, Jones didn't get through. I knew he wouldn't," said the Very Young Mason, sitting down in the anteroom.

"Zat so?" the Old Tiler made answer, hitching his sword more comfortably. "Some of you young Masons sure do know a lot."

"Well, I knew he wouldn't get through because I know two brethren who were going to black-ball him," defended the Very Young Mason.

"Oh, well, I have heard of that before, too. Don't tell me who your friends were. I don't want to know them. They are probably good fellows and perhaps they try, once in a while, to be good Masons. But they don't succeed very well."

"Why, what do you mean? They are splendid fellows, both of them. They know this fellow Jones ought not to be made a member and so they keep him out. One of them is——"

"Wait a minute, Son, wait a minute. I am not objecting to your friends because they blackballed a candidate. That is their inalienable right. I am objecting to their having told you what they were going to do. The secrecy of the ballot is one of the great guardians of the Masonic fraternity. Every brother has a right to vote as his conscience tells him he should. None has the right to tell others either how they will vote or how they have voted. Whoever does so, tears down in small measure, perhaps, but to some extent, the fraternity to which he belongs. If every

Forty-eight

Mason told how he would or had balloted, there would be no secret ballot. Take away the secret ballot and Masonry loses her guardian—for the moment the ballot is controlled by outside influence that moment Masonry is no longer under the guidance of the hearts of its members.

"If I know you will vote against my candidate, I argue with you. I plead with you. I remind you of the favor I did you. I work upon your feeling and perhaps, for my sake, you let into the lodge a man I like but whom you believe unfit for membership. If I don't know how you will vote, I cannot argue with you, and your vote is dictated, as it should be, entirely by your conscience."

"But——"

"Never mind the 'but' just yet. Let's finish this. After my candidate gets in, because of your affection for me, in spite of your knowledge of his unfitness, then what? Isn't the lodge weaker than it was? Even if you are mistaken and a good man thus gets in, isn't your feeling that he isn't a good man a weakening influence in the lodge? Are you not apt to value it a little less because you weakened it? The harm, once done, may persist for years—and all because you opened your mouth and let out a few words of your intentions before you balloted."

"But suppose I want advice as to how to ballot? How can I come to you and ask your advice without telling you what I think I should do?"

"You can't. But there is a remedy made and provided for just such cases. Masonry in its wisdom demands that every application be investigated by a committee for a month prior to the ballot. His name is placed before you. You have ample time to go to the committee. If you know anything you can prove, it is your duty to tell them. If you don't know, but have heard something against the applicant, turn over what you have heard to the committee. Let the committee find the facts. If there are no facts—if what you heard is idle rumor—the committee will find it out. If there is foundation to the gossip, they will find that out. Then you be guided by what the committee reports.

"Oh, but that is to say that all the balloting should be done by the committee."

"Not at all, not at all," answered the Old Tiler. "You let your committee decide for you as to the foundation of the rumor or the malice behind the gossip. If you know anything which in your mind justifies a blackball your course and your conscience are clear. Your question was as to what you should do when you needed advice.

"But committees are often so perfunctory."

"That's your fault!" was the immediate and sharp answer.

"My fault? How you make that out?"

"If you think a committee has made a perfunctory investigation, tell the Master you would like to have a new committee appointed. If you think a committee isn't doing its duty, go to its members and ask them what they have found out and what they have done. If they won't tell you, notify the Master that you wish more time. He won't refuse it, he knows that such a request means a blackball if it is refused. No good Master wants any good man kept out, or any unfit man let in. And finally, get yourself on a few committees—the Master will be happy to have your request for such work. Then, by example, show the other committees what a real committee can do. Any lodge which has poor or perfunctory committees has only its individual members to blame."

"I see," said the Young Mason. "I wonder why all this isn't told to us when we come into the lodge for the first time?"

"Hump. 'All this.' Boy, there are literally hundreds of thousands of books written about Masonry. Do you expect some one to come to you and teach you the contents of them all? The shoe is on the other foot."

"How you mean, other foot?"

"When you first came into the lodge, why didn't you ask?" responded the Old Tiler, tersely, as he rose to answer raps on the door.

On the Book on the Altar

"I HEARD the most curious tale," began the New Member, seating himself beside the Old Tiler during refreshment.

"Shoot!" commanded the Old Tiler.

"Friend of mine belongs to a Mid-West lodge. Seems they elected a chap to become a member but when he took the degree he stopped the work to ask for the Koran in place of the Bible on the altar. Said he wanted the Holy Book of his faith, and the Bible wasn't it!"

"Yes, yes; go on," prompted the Old Tiler. "What did they do?"

"The officers held a pow-wow and the Master finally decided that as the ritual demanded the 'Holy Bible, Square and Compasses' as furniture for the lodge, the applicant was wrong and that he'd have to use the Bible or not take his degree. And the funny part of it all was that the initiate was quite satisfied and took his degree with the Bible on the altar. I'm glad they have him, and not this lodge."

"Why?"

"Why, a chap who backs down that way can't have very much courage; I'd have had more respect for him if he'd insisted and if he couldn't have his way, refused to go on with the degree."

"All wrong, Brother, all wrong!" commented the Old Tiler. "The Mohammedan initiate wasn't concerned about himself but about the lodge. He showed a high degree of knowledge of Masonic principles in asking for his own Holy Book, and a great consideration for the lodge. Think a minute. This man isn't a Christian. He doesn't believe in Christ or the Christian God. He believes in Allah, and Mohammed as his prophet. The Bible, to you a Holy Book, is to him no more than the Koran is to you. You wouldn't regard an obligation taken on a dictionary or a cook book or a Koran as binding, in the same degree that you would one taken on the Bible.

"That's the way this chap felt. He wanted to take his obligation in such a way that it would bind his conscience. And the Master would not let him, because he slavishly and narrow-mindedly followed the words of the ritual instead of the spirit of Masonry.

"Masonry does not limit an applicant to his choice of a name for a Supreme Being. I can believe in Allah, or Buddha, or Confucius or Mithra, or Christ, or Siva, or Brahma, or Jehovah, and be a good Mason. If I believe in a Supreme Being, a Great Architect, that is all Masonry demands of me; my brethren do not care what I name Him."

"Then you think this chap isn't really obligated? I must write my friend and warn him ____"

"Softly, softly. I didn't say that. Any man with enough reverence for Masonry, in advance of knowledge of it, to want to stop a degree to get his own Holy Book on which to take an obligation, in order to protect the lodge he sought to join, would feel himself morally obligated to keep his word, whether there was his, another's or no Holy Book at all, on the altar. You know, my

Fifty-three

brother, that an oath is not really binding because of the book beneath your hand when you swear. It is the spirit within you, with which you assume an obligation, which makes it binding. The Book is but a symbol that you do here and now, in the presence of the God you revere, make your promise. The cement of brotherly love which we spread is not material—the working tools of a Master Mason are not used upon stone but upon human hearts. Your brother did his best to conform to the spirit of our usages in asking for the Book he had been taught to revere. Failing in that, through no fault of his own, I make no doubt he took his obligation with a sincere belief in its sacredness. But legally, of course, he would not be considered to commit perjury if he asked for his own Book and was forced to use another.

"What's the law got to do with it?"

"Just nothing at all—which is the point I make. In England and America, Canada and South America, Australia, and part of the Continent, the Bible is almost universally used. In Scottish bodies you will find many Holy Books; they don't wait to be asked for them. But let me ask you this, when our ancient brethren met on hills and in valleys, long before Christ gave the Christian religion to the world, did they use the New Testament on their altars? Of course not; there was none. You can say, if you will, that they used the old, and I can say they used a Talmud and someone else can say they used none at all, and one of us is as right as another. But they used a reverence for sacred things.

"If you will write your friend, you might tell him that any ritual which permits a man to name his God as he pleases, but demands that a Book which reveres one particular God, be used, is faulty. The ritual of Masonry *is* faulty; it was made by man. But the Spirit of Masonry is divine; it comes, not from men's minds but from their hearts. If matters of obligation and books and names of Deity are matters of the spirit, every possible condition is satisfied. If I were Master and an applicant demanded any one, or any six books on which to lay his hand while he pledged himself to us, I'd get 'em if they were to be had, and I'd tell my lodge what a thoughtful, reverent, Masonic spirit was in the man who asked."

"Seems to me you believe in a lot of funny things; how many Gods do you believe in?"

"There is but One," was the Old Tiler's answer, "call Him what you will. Let me repeat a little bit of verse for you:

"At the Meuzzin's call for prayer
The kneeling faithful thronged the square;
Amid a monastery's weeds,
An old Franciscan told his beads,
While on Pushkara's lofty height
A dark priest chanted Brahma's might,
While to the synagogue there came
A Jew, to praise Jehovah's Name.

"The One Great God looked down and smiled
And counted each His loving child;
For Turk and Brahmin, monk and Jew
Had reached Him through the Gods they knew."

"If we reach Him at all in Masonry, it makes little difference by what sacred Name we arrive," finished the Old Tiler, reverently.

"You've reached me, anyhow," said the New Brother, shaking hands as if he meant it.

On the Helping Hand

"I AM very much disappointed in it," said the New Brother, sadly, as he sat down beside the Old Tiler during refreshment.

"Disappointed in what?" asked the wielder of the sword.

"Why, Masonry in general, and this lodge in particular," answered the New Brother. "Neither are what I thought they were."

"That's too bad," sympathized the Old Tiler. "Tell me about it."

"Well, my dad was a Mason and he was always talking about how helpful Masonry was and how a lodge stood back of a fellow, and how one brother would go out of his way to help another, and how, when you were in trouble, a brother would come and help you out of it. And I believed it. But I have been a member here now for some time, and I haven't seen any of that."

"Been in trouble, Son?" asked the Old Tiler.

"I suppose everyone has some troubles."

"But have you been in any real trouble, where you would have been aided by the lodge had the lodge known of it?"

"That isn't the question," answered the New Brother.

"No, I'll agree it isn't. So I will ask you the real question," said the Old Tiler, and his lips lost their smile as he spoke. "How many brothers have you helped during the time you have been a member? How many shoulders have you slapped, how many men have you gone to and said, 'Jim, I know you are in trouble, count on me to help because we both belong to the same lodge?'"

"Why, how you talk!" replied the New Brother. "Why, I hardly know any one in lodge, yet. How would I know whether they were in trouble?"

"The same way they would know if you were in trouble, of course!" answered the Old Tiler. "Listen to me, Son, because I am an old man and I have had a lot of trouble, most of which never happened. You complain that Masonry is a failure because you have not personally experienced its helping hand. You admit you haven't needed it. And you also admit you haven't held it out. Let me tell you that brotherhood means the relation between brothers, not the relation of one brother to another and no come-back. If you can't be a brother, you can't expect a man to be a brother to you. You ask me how you would know if a brother is in trouble. How does anyone know? Lem'me tell you a few stories I heard this last week. Brother A, of this lodge, lost his wife two weeks ago. It was in the papers. Two brothers of this lodge sent their wives to his house to look after his children until he could make arrangements for a nurse. Another brother of this lodge failed in business. This lodge took no lodge action because it wasn't necessary, but two bankers and a business man went to the poor failure and staked him, and put him on his feet. A brother of this lodge has a boy who is wild. Last week the boy went joy-riding with too much hooch in him and smashed up a car which didn't belong to him. The owner was going to put the boy in jail, where he belonged, but a brother of this lodge went to him and took the responsibility on himself, sent the boy to a farm during good behavior, saved a father from having a broken heart and maybe saved society from a criminal. A brother of this lodge had his house burn down last month. It wasn't insured. He had just paid for it. Ten brothers of this lodge financed his new house, and he will pay for it at the rate of a dollar a week for life, or something; but he had fraternal help.

"There are three brothers in the lodge now, out of work, and without a dollar in their clothes. Before they go away to-night I'll bet it gets known and some one will see that they get a chance."

"But how do brothers know other brothers are in trouble? They don't get up in lodge and tell it."

"How did you expect people were going to come and help you if you didn't let 'em know you needed help?" countered the Old Tiler.

"Why, I dunno—I just thought maybe someone would have enough interest in me to know ——"

"Well, have you had enough interest in your brethren to know when they were in trouble?"

"I—er—why——"

"You needn't answer. Now lemme tell you something else, Son. In every part of the world there are the 'gimme's' and the 'lemme's.' The 'gimme's' are those who want things done, and the 'lemme's' are the fellows who do them. In every part of the world are the 'haves' and the 'haven'ts.' In every Masonic lodge are a lot of 'haves' and a few 'haven'ts.' It's up to the 'haves' to share with the 'haven'ts'; I take it you are naturally a 'have.' You have money, clothes, a good position. You are not in need of help from your brother. But a lot of your brethren are in need of help from you. It may be a dollar, it may be some advice, it may be a word to an influential friend, it may be a loan, it may be just some of the things I have told you about. If brotherhood is to mean to you what you expected it would, it won't be because you get it, but because you give it. A Masonic lodge is not, and should never be to any man if he can help it, a place or an organization from which he expects to get something. It ought to be a place or an organization in which he expects to have the beautiful opportunity to put something. If everyone was disappointed and everyone said it was a failure because no one did anything, it would be a failure. It isn't a failure because most real Masons look for the chance to do something for some brother who needs help."

"Some brethren do a lot for idiotic new members, just by talking to them!" responded the New Brother remorsefully. "Say, do you suppose you could slip a dollar to each of those three who haven't any and tell 'em you found it on the floor?"

"I shouldn't wonder," answered the Old Tiler.

"And will you please believe I don't think it's a failure and the only thing about it which is disappointing to me is myself?"

"Uh-huh," answered the Old Tiler.

On Being in Step

"THANK you for tiling," said the Old Tiler, as he resumed his sword after a trip to the ice-water stand. "What they doing in there now?"

"Oh, fighting like a lot of snarling puppies!" responded the Young Mason, disgustedly. "My idea of Masonry is not a red-hot discussion on the floor every meeting, as to whether or not Jim Jones is or isn't, or we ought or ought not, to spend eleven dollars for something or other.

"No? Well, go on; tell us what your idea of Masonry is!" and the Old Tiler tried his best to keep his voice from being sardonic.

But the Young Mason had bumped up against the keen Old Tiler before. "Not much I won't, and have you blow my ideas full of air holes!" he retorted. "But I would like you to tell me why some lodges are such units, pull so well together, have such a harmonious conception of themselves and their goal, and others, like this of ours, are always fighting."

"Humph!" answered the Old Tiler. "Did you ever see a dog fight with only one dog? You did not. Did you ever see a boiler explode without too much steam and not enough water in it? You did not. Did you ever see a team of horses take a heavy load uphill when they all pulled different ways? You did not.

"Lodges are like all these things—a lodge can't fight unless it has something to quarrel about.

The reason we are having a series of floor fusses inside is because we have about three or eleven alleged brothers who haven't managed to learn anything about military drill! If they went into the National Guard they'd hear an old drill sergeant say, 'hep, hep, hep,' a few thousand times, and after a while they'd get 'hep' to themselves and their neighbors. At first they'd be like the soldier son of the proud old Irish mother who watched her boy parade, and told her friend, 'Ah, do yez moind, they wuz all out o' step but him!' But after a while they'd learn that they couldn't keep in step just by going as they pleased—they'd know they must watch the fellow to the right and the chap to the left, in order to stay in step.

"Well, in a lodge there are brothers who won't stay in step, not because they can't, but because they are too busy watching their own steps to watch the other fellow. Take Biggsby, now—Biggsby is that big fellow with the overgrown grip on a nickle, who is forever and always blocking business by insisting on a detailed explanation of every appropriation. He isn't in step. This lodge of ours is big enough and rich enough to spend some money witthout worrying. Biggsby has an idea that if we don't pinch ten cent pieces until they drip coppers, we are going to go to the Masonic Home!"

"But," interrupted the Young Mason, "isn't it right to have someone watch the appropriations?"

"Sure it is," answered the Old Tiler, "watch 'em by all means, and raise merry ned if anyone tries to slip something over. But watching 'em is one thing and objecting to the wishes of the majority because one happens to have private beliefs regarding the sacredness of two-bit pieces is another. No one cares if Biggsby wants to wear out a dollar's worth of shoes saving a five-cent car ride because they are Biggsby's shoes and that's Biggsby's business. But when he comes into lodge, he ought to get in step with the lodge, and not block things by objecting to lodge expenditures on personal grounds.

"Then there is the matter of politics. Don't tell me there should be no politics in Masonry—I know it, just as I know there never was a lodge yet that didn't have politics in its elections, same as it has ballots in the ballot box. It's the nature of the beast; but when Jim Jones lobbies around tryin to get Bob Smith elected, and Frank Robinson spends good time and effort trying to get Bill Brown elected, no special harm is done, unless they all keep up their fight after it is won and lost! 'Some people never know when they are licked,' is not always a compliment. In a lodge with real lodge spirit, when Bill loses his fight, he forgets it, and roots and works for the successful candidate. In a lodge where Bill isn't 'hep' either to his mates, his Masonry or himself, he carries a grouch, tries to make the successful chap unhappy, gets in the way of the machinery and generally stirs up trouble.

"Now, boy, you are just beginning in Masonry. You have joined a darn good lodge. What's happening in there is just a phase. Those fellows will learn, in time, that when ten or forty or four hundred men form a real Masonic lodge, as a body they are something bigger and better than jus ten or forty or four hundred times the bigness and goodness of the individuals. When a lodge has a true lodge spirit, there is a lot of give and not much take. When every member of a lodge is 'hep' to the other fellow and his ideas—when every member who comes to a meeting makes a very careful distinction between his ideas of conduct for himself and what his organization should do—when each and every one of us tries to think of his fellow-member as his brother in blood, in heart, in hope, and love, as well as in organization, then and not until then, does your lodge develop real lodge spirit and stop foolish fighting. See?"

"I see," answered the Young Mason. "I get it that a lodge is like a piece of machinery—if it isn't well oiled, it squeaks, and if any one part of is is out of order, the whole suffers. And because we Masons are just human beings, we are not apt to be perfect and so no lodge is ever perfect. But at that we can make our lodges a lot better than they are by sinking some of our individual desires for the good of the organization."

"Well, well!" said the Old Tiler. "Almost do you persuade me you have the makings of a real good——"

But just then there were three raps, and the Young Mason is still wondering whether the Old Tiler meant to say "fellow" or "Mason" or "officer!"

On Defending Masonry

"SAY, Old Timer, tell me something," began the New Member.

"It's a rainy evening," answered the Old Tiler.

"Huh?"

"I said it was a rainy evening. You asked me to tell you something."

"Oh, I mean something about how a Mason ought to behave. Last night I was at a party—little neighborhood gathering. And a couple of women commenced to ask me questions about Masonry. Then a couple of fellows chimed in. And there was a Mason present and he kept putting them off and telling them fairy tales and showing them 'signs,' like wiggling his fingers at his ears, and generally kidding them. Then one of the men who wasn't a Mason told what he had been told by Masons about Masonry and it was the greatest hodgepodge of truth and fancy! So I——"

"So you cut in and told them all the truth you dared tell them without breaking your obligation!"

"Exactly. How did you know?"

"Why, Son, I was a new member myself, once. It's a long, long time ago, but I haven't forgotten. I, too, used to think myself the champion of Masonry. I, too, used to rush in, and explain, and talk, and discourse, and try to put the fraternity in a good light before the profane. We all do—until we learn better.

"Why, what do you mean? Shouldn't I have talked?"

"You should not," answered the Old Tiler. "Son, Masonry is so much bigger than you are, than your friends are, than any one is, that it's like a towering mountain at the base of which some puppies play. Imagine the puppies getting into a discussion about the mountain!

"Says the short-tailed pup, 'the mountain is really hollow and filled with green cheese.' Says the long-tailed pup, 'yes, and all the rats in the world live on the green cheese and play tag through the holes they eat in it.' Whereupon the old dog, who belongs to the society of the mountain says, 'the mountain is a huge pile of earth, has no green cheese in it, and no rats. Its principal function is to supply a hilly place for big dogs to run up and down and get exercise!'

"Would it make very much difference to the mountain? Hardly. And it makes no difference to Masonry that a few misunderstand it, or make jokes about it. There will always be those who consider that it is funny to talk about the 'goat' and who like to make foolish people laugh by wiggling their fingers over their ears and talking about 'signs.' But that doesn't hurt Masonry. What does hurt it is Masons, such as you may become, rushing in to defend that which needs no defense."

"But why should I let those women have false ideas? They said they heard that we did nothing but play cards in lodge!"

Sixty-five

"What of it. If you said you heard that people did nothing but play cards at a church service, would it hurt the church? Anyone who ever went to church would know you were a foolish boy, repeating something that wasn't so. But the minister who wasted his time going around assuring people no one played cards in his church, when he might be teaching the Word, would be a poor preacher. If people say we play cards in lodge it doesn't hurt us. It does hurt us if we discuss lodge matters in public. Look wise, say nothing. Masonry is for Masons. What the profane say of us is often untrue, frequently unkind, always uninformed. And it injures us just as the puppies saying the mountain is made of cheese injures the mountain. Son, don't shoot off your face."

"But am I never to mention Masonry to any one?"

"No—not unless they mention it to you, and then only to answer an honest question if you can. If a man says, "tell me something of Masonry, what it is, and for what it stands,' that is an honest inquiry and deserves an honest answer. Tell him Masonry is a fraternity teaching great truths, trying to make men better, helping civilization march onward by emphasizing the brotherhood of man and the fatherhood of God. Then shut up. If he asks you how he may be a Mason, tell him, 'by asking a brother for a petition and following instructions.' If he says, 'I want to be a Mason, how shall I proceed?' that is a direct query which concerns you. If you want him in your lodge, then, and not until then, can you legally offer him the privilege of making petition to your lodge.

"The great stronghold of Masonry in the hearts of men is its vital truth. But the regard in which Masonry is held by the general public is due to its reticence, to its reserve, its quiet, unostentatious way of doing, its failure to advertise, its lack of the brass band and the tooting horn. You can do nothing in your little circle better calculated to impress them with the dignity of the fraternity, the value of its teachings, the worth of its principles, then by remaining silent, by refusing to discuss it; by practicing those truly Masonic virtues, silence and circumspection.

"An ass, my brother, is known by the loudness of his bray. A donkey is known by his stubbornness. A woman is known by her modesty and a good Mason by his reverent regard for the principles of his great order and his ability to keep his mouth shut.

"The curiosity seeker, the idle inquiry, the fun-making thrust, the alleged 'expose' of Masonry are everywhere. Remember the Sabbath Day to keep it holy can be also rendered, 'Remember the Altar, to keep it sacred.' And he who keeps his Masonic Altar sacred in his heart will find no need to defend it before the vulgar or speak of it, save privately, and to the honest inquirer."

"You ought to have been a grand master!" said the New Member.

"No," answered the Old Tiler, "they also serve who only stand and tile."

"And talk hard sense to foolish new members!" said the New Member, gratefully.

On Reasons for Wanting to Be a Mason

"I THINK Jones is a nut!" remarked the New Brother to the Old Tiler. "I went with him yesterday to look up a chap who has applied for membership. Of course, I didn't know much about such things, so I let him do the talking. And the questions that man asked!"

"Yes? Why, what did he say?"

"Well, the first thing he wanted to know was what kind of a job the applicant held, how long he had been there, where he had worked before, was he satisfied, did he like his boss, how much he made and whether he saved any of it or spent it all!"

"Quite right, too," commented the Old Tiler. "He asked those questions to find out whether the applicant was a solid citizen, able to pay his dues and not likely to become a charge on the lodge. A 'floater,' one of these chaps who holds a job to-day and leaves it to-morrow for another is always apt to be an applicant for charity."

"But that's one of the things a lodge is for—charity," said the New Brother.

"The lodge is for charity to its members who are in need, yes," answered the Old Tiler. "But no lodge willingly takes in members who may need charity. Masonry is not a crutch for the indigent. It is a staff for those who go lame in life's journey, but when a chap starts out lame he has to get crutches from some other institution."

"Well, then he asked some more strange questions. For instance, he asked, 'Why do you want to become a Mason?' Now, that seemed to me to be an impertinence. A man's reasons for wanting to join Masonry are surely his own and no business of ours."

"Is that so!" answered the Old Tiler. "Son, you know so many things that are not so! I have been on the petitions of a great many men and that is always my first question. I have heard a great many answers, too. Some men want to join because their father was a Mason. Some think it will help them along in life. Some very frankly say they want to make friends so they can be successful. Others think that Masonry will help them in their religion. Still others want to be Masons because they want to belong to a secret society."

"Well, I don't see that it's any business of ours."

"It is, just the same. A man who wants to join a fraternity because his father belonged, is good material. He wants to imitate his father. That his father was a Mason is evidence that his father was a good man. If the applicant desires to imitate a good man, and thinks we can help him, his motives are worthy. But the man who wants to become a Mason because he thinks Masonry will stiffen his religious belief is not a good candidate. Masonry demands no religion of its applicants, merely a belief in Deity. But when a man has religious convictions which are slipping back and looks for something to prop them up, he should go elsewhere than to the Masonic altar. Asking nothing but a belief in God, we have a

Sixty-nine

right to demand that that belief be strong, well grounded, unshakable, and beyond question.

"The man who says he wants to join the Masonic order because he wants to belong to a secret society doesn't get asked any more questions! He is 'killed' right there. Masonry is no haven for curiosity seekers. The chap who thinks Masonry will make him friends who will help him in his business gets nowhere with a good committee. Masonry is not a business club. Imagine a man going to a minister and saying: 'I want to join your church so I can sell lawn mowers to your members.' Would the minister want him? He would not. Masonry is not a church, but it is holy to Masons; surely you know by now that Masonry is a bright and shining light in a man's heart and that the lamp must not be sullied by profane motives. To attempt to use Masonry for business purposes is like using the Bible to sit on —diverting from the proper purpose that which should be held sacred.

"The man who answers that question by saying, 'I have always heard of Masons as men who receive real help in being good men; I would like to have the privilege of becoming a member,' is approaching the matter in the right spirit. Masonry doesn't hunt the man, the man must hunt the lodge. And he must hunt with a pure motive, or he can not join this or any good lodge, with a good committee. The motive is important, vitally important. We want to know if he is married and has children, because, if so, we must dig still deeper to find out if he can afford to become a Mason. Some people can't afford $50 for a fee and $5 a year for dues. If they have to rob their children or their wives to join we have no use for them. We want to know if a man stands well with his fellows outside the lodge; if he does, he is apt to stand well with them inside. If he has few friends and those of doubtful character, outside the lodge, the chances are he is not good timber for the lodge.

"Never forget, my son, that Masonry is what we make it. Every good man and true who comes into a lodge helps the fraternity to be bigger, better, nobler. Every insincere man, every scoffer, every dishonest man who gets into lodge, by so much injures the fraternity. Masonry can accomplish good in the hearts of men only as it is bigger and better than they are. When it becomes less good than the average man, the average man will not want to join, and its power will be gone.

"The price of liberty, so we are told, is eternal vigilance. The price of quality in a lodge is eternal care on the part of the investigation committee. It is an important job and should be approached with the idea that the weight of the future of the lodge, in particular, and Masonry in general, to some extent rests on the man making the investigation."

"Hm. Thanks. See you later."

"You're welcome—but what is your hurry?"

"Got to find Jones and tell him I'm the nut— and ask him to let me go with him again and see if I can't see something else in his questions besides foolishness!" answered the New Brother.

On Costumes

"THEY are having a hot old discussion in there," replied the New Brother to the Old Tiler's inquiry. "Jones is on his feet arguing his head off that we ought to spend $500 of $1000 for costumes for the degrees. Past Master Smith is marshalling all his forces to combat it."

"Yes, that's the way it would line up. Harry Jones hopes he will be master in a couple of years and wants costumes, and Smith, of course, doesn't want his last year's record eclipsed."

"Well, I'm against costumes," said the New Brother. "Looks like a waste of money to me."

"Is that so! Brother, why is it waste?"

"Why, we can confer the degrees just as well without them."

"Yes, and wouldn't we be able to confer the degrees just as well in a plain board building as in a fine Masonic Temple, before brethren seated on wooden boxes as well as on expensively upholstered leather settees, and by candle light as well as by electric light?"

"Oh, well! Of course we want to be comfortable and to impress the candidate——"

"But that is what costumes are for, to impress the candidate. The degrees of Masonry are allegorical; they teach lessons of the present from happenings of the past. Any way we can make them more impressive, must make the lesson easier to learn, and so better learned," countered the Old Tiler, but he wore an odd little smile as he spoke.

"You can't tell me———"

"Oh, yes, I can. I am telling you. When we put on a third degree in costume we take the candidate back to the building of the Temple. We show him characters dressed as characters used to dress. He finds in the story a reality which he cannot get if the actors are dressed in modern clothes. The story is impressive only as it impresses. The more real it is, the more potent the impression. Costumes add largely to the spectacular features of the degree.

"I guess you are right, at that," answered the New Brother. "You certainly argue well. I guess I'll support Jones in his costume idea."

"Oh, I wouldn't do that!" The Old Tiler was grinning broadly now. "You haven't thought the question out yet."

"But you have just argued me into believing in costumes," answered the New Brother, bewildered.

"Oh, no, I haven't. I have just told you what the costume proponents say of it. But there is another side. Masonry is a system of philosophy taught by allegories and symbols. We are not really stone masons. We do not actually cut stone or lay mortar or build actual buildings. Our Masonry is speculative, not operative. But the legend of our third degree is, when put on in costume, certainly an operative, not a speculative performance. The aprons we wear in lodge would hardly do for a real worker in stone; they are but imitations, symbols, of his body protector and tool holder. Our lodge room does not look like the exterior of a temple, and the three gates are represented but by imagination. Why put the actors in costumes and omit the scenery? If we are going to have costumes, why not have a stage and lights and scenery and everything?"

"I don't know why not," said the New Brother, thoughtfully.

"Well, that's because there isn't any reason why not," answered the Old Tiler. "Some lodges do it that way. But the vast majority do not. The majority of lodges have no stages, no costumes and no real actors. The majority of lodges have earnest degree workers, who go through the degree with the Masonic idea of instructing the candidate in one of the greatest lessons which one man can teach another; a lesson so great that it does not need costumes. When the minister stands in the pulpit to read the gospel, does he act the parts of those whose words he reads? There is but one Passion Play, but all Christianity knows the story. It needs no costumes to sink home to the heart.

"So it is with the Masonic story. It needs no trappings to be glorious. It needs no bright and yellow and blue robe to be effective. It carries its own dignity, by its own impressiveness. To put a business man in a blue and green robe and tell him he is to act like a stone mason of the time of Solomon, without scenery or training, is not to add to the impressiveness of the degree, but to take away from it."

"I guess you are right," said the New Brother, thoughtfully. "I guess I will go in there and uphold Brother Smith in his contention that we don't need the costumes."

"But we do need them!" countered the Old Tiler.

"But you have just argued me into thinking we should not buy them!"

"Not at all, not at all," was the smiling answer. "I have just quoted you the reasons some urge against them."

"But one side must be right and one side wrong!" protested the New Brother.

"Oh, no. It's not a matter of sides but of men. Listen, son, till I tell you. The degree neither needs costumes, nor needs to be put on without them. But some men do need costumes in which to work; others don't. The right answer is the people who are to work the degree. A group of men who are dramatic, who are actors, who throw themselves into the story as if it were a play, will do better work if that fiction is made real to them, with costumes. A group of men who find the story an allegory, rather than a play, will do better without them. Both ways, in costume and in dress suits, are good. It depends on the men who do the work.

"Well, I know what I am going to do," said the New Brother. "I am going back in that lodge and vote whichever way the degree team votes!"

"You see," answered the Old Tiler, "I *did* manage to tell you!"

On "Pepping Up the Lodge"

"IT'S a wonderful idea! I'm strong for it, strong!" said the New Brother to the Old Tiler, coming out into the anteroom for air.

"Tell me about it," suggested the Old Tiler. "Wonderful ideas are rare in a lodge."

"Well, you see, a lot of us have been thinking the old lodge needs pepping up. We go along in the same old way, never doing much of anything different; just making Masons and having little lodgeroom talks and all, and so we thought—Smitty and Bunny and Wilmot and a few others and I—that we'd start something. So we plan to hire a boat and take the lodge down the river and have a special dispensation and hold a third degree and feed out on the water. We are going to hire a band, all Masons, of course, and probably have an entertainment afterwards; maybe we can get some high divers and hold a swimming race, too."

"I'll say it's a wonderful idea," commented the Old Tiler, "but you don't carry it far enough.

"Well, I thought maybe you could help me add to it," said the New Brother, enthusiastically. "What would you suggest?"

"Well, I think a small boat in the river is undignified. Why not hire an ocean liner? Why not go half way to Europe, and instead of having diving and swimming matches, get a couple of whales and have a real whale of a time? Or you might get Uncle Sam to lend you a couple of submarines. And I wouldn't hire just a Masonic band. Get three or eleven bands, and have a band competition; see which can blow the loudest. Hold all three of the degrees at once; the first in the hold, the second on deck and third up in the crow's nest. This would be different and exhilarating. Don't be a piker! If you are going to innovate, innovate *right!*"

"Why, you are laughing at me! Don't you think it's a good idea to put pep in the lodge? Didn't the Shriners hold an initiation in Luray Cave, and another in the locks at the canal, and didn't our ancient brethren hold their lodges on hills and in valleys and——

"Yep. The Shrine did, and does, and will again, more power to it. The Shrine is a modern organization, with no need to uphold ancient traditions. The Shrine is a fun-loving organization, the playground for Masonry and Masons; it thrives on the new, the different, the novel, the startling. I love the Shrine, and everything it does. I love a good comedy, too, but I don't like to see a minister pulling funny stuff in the pulpit. And what is fine for the Shrine is poor for the lodge.

"Our ancient brethren held their meetings on hills and in valleys; they had no buildings. Had we no temples we could and would do the same. But our ancient brethren didn't go out under the stars to be 'peppy,' nor should we.

"Somewhere or other in Shakespeare (I think it's Henry IV) are the lines, 'Fickle changelings and poor discontents, which gape and rub elbow at the news of hurly-burly innovations.' There are fickle men in lodge who tire of the beauties of Freemasonry and would, indeed, make 'hurly-burly innovations.' There are 'poor discontented' ones who are never satisfied unless they are being amused, but they are neither devout church-goers nor devoted lodge members.

"No, I can't say much for your idea. To me, trying to put 'pep' into Masonic degrees is like painting a statue or putting perfume on a flower, or having red fire and a brass band at a funeral.

"To me, Masonry is something solemn and sacred and beautiful. It is beautiful with age, age that has mellowed and softened it, and given it the tints and colors of glory of service. Would you improve the Grand Canyon with better colors than nature gave it? How can you improve a lodge meeting with a boat, a brass band and a diving contest? Masonry, to me, is sacred; it is holy, as the dear and inner things of the spirit are holy. When you go on your knees to your Creator, do you play the phonograph, dance a jig and tell a funny story to put 'pep' in the performance?

"Masonry is much more than lodge meetings; it is selflessness, brotherhood, charity, toleration, veneration; it is the sweet and quiet influence which makes a brother more than a mere lodge member; it is an expression of the divine will to make men better. You cannot aid it with a boat trip or a brass band, my son; you cannot help it by innovations. You must take it or leave it as it is; that which has endured for centuries needs no such artificial stimulation."

Seventy-eight

"But don't you believe in entertainment or excursions or play?" asked the New Brother.

"Ah! That is something else again! Hire a boat, get a band, hold a diving contest, make merry, by all means. Have a lodge picnic, blowout, whatever you will, and I'll help you do it. But don't spoil the picnic by trying to make it into a lodge meeting, and don't spoil a good meeting by trying to make a picnic out of it.

"By all means do I believe in picnics and outings. We are taught to have refreshment. But we are not taught to try to mix labor and refreshment. And we are taught that it is the first of the ancient laws that it is beyond the power of any Mason to change the ancient laws. Now, you find me any authority in the ancient laws for holding a third degree in a boat with a brass band and a diving contest and I'll help you do it! Otherwise, I'll try to keep the old lodge just as she is and save the pep you want to put in the solemn and reverent business of Masonry for the excursion you want to give and don't know it!"

"I do know it now," said the New Brother. "Something tells me this proposition will not be popular if I bring it up in lodge, unless I make it plain it's an excursion and not an attempt to put 'pep' in the degrees."

"Something tells you right, Son," answered the Old Tiler.

On Being a Committeeman

"I DON'T think it's right to give one brother so much to do!" protested one New Brother, displaying to the Old Tiler reports on petitioners. He held three in his hands. "Here I am, a busy man. And in place of sending three reports to three different brethren, they give 'em all to me. Yet the other two investigators on each petition are different. I am the only one who gets three to look up. But I know what I can do. Jones, who is on one of these petitions, is a careful chap; I'll ask him and do as he says. And Smith, who is on the second one, always digs into a petitioner's qualifications. I'll just see what he says. And the third chap I think I can investigate myself, by telephone. Don't know as all that is so much work, after all."

"No, it isn't, not that way. The lodge will be real proud of you," said the Old Tiler. "When you tell them the way you have done their work, they will hang the leather medal on your neck."

"Well, you don't see me getting up and telling them, do you?" asked the New Brother. "I never heard of a committeeman telling the lodge how he worked."

"If he really works, he doesn't have to tell them!" answered the Old Tiler. "If he loafs, and is faithless to his trust, betraying the brethren who trusted him, of course he wouldn't want to tell them."

"Are you insinuating that I would be faithless to a trust?" demanded the New Brother, fiercely.

"Well, you can call it insinuating if you want to," answered the Old Tiler. "But I didn't mean to insinuate. I meant to say it right out. Any man who investigates a petition in the way you have indicated, is betraying the brethren who trusted him, is injuring the lodge which made him a Master Mason, is faithless to his trust. I don't see anything 'insinuating' about that—I think it's a plain, straight-from-the-shoulder statement!

"Listen to me, New Brother, and listen hard, because what I am going to say is for the good of your soul though you won't like it. Masonry is cursed with laziness, like any other human institution; the church, the school, the government, are all less effective than they might be, because men are lazy. If the lodge paid you a $10 bill for your report you'd scorn to take the service. But the lodge doesn't pay you; it merely trusts you to do your work for those 'masters wages' which you have sworn to earn. And when you refuse to do the work, though agreeing with the lodge that you will do it, you are cheating.

"The body of Masonry is the men who compose the order. As those men are well-chosen, God-fearing, upright, honest men, so will the order be powerful, able to do good in the world which sadly needs of it, function to some purpose. If those men are weak, vicious, ineffective, so will the order be ineffective, vicious and weak. There are millions of men who are Masons, and some of them are the wrong men. Never a church but has some unworthy members, never a government but has some venal officials, and

Eighty-one

never the Masonic lodge which did not have some members the other members would rather not have as brethren. In the government and the church there is more excuse; the government is large, and changing, and control of details is injured by politics; the church must open her doors to the just and the unjust alike. But the Masonic lodge with the wrong men as Masons has only the Masonic lodge to blame; it must blame itself because it picked the lazy and the inefficient as committeemen.

"Man, as committeeman you have the lodge in your keeping. In effect the lodge has said to you, 'in your hands, my brother, do we put our reputation. As you labor, so shall we prosper. As you forget, lie down, are lazy on the job, so shall we suffer. The reputation of Masonry is in your hands; see that you keep it unsullied.'

"And you talk about taking some other man's say-so, about using the telephone, about 'too much work.' It is not work the lodge has given you, it is an honor which has been conferred upon you. It is not effort they are asking of you, it is a favor they have done you. The lodge has said to you, 'We trust you. Choose for us wisely. Let no man approach our altar who is not fit to tend the holy fire. Let no man within our doors who is not meet and proper for the benefits of Masonry, who will not reflect credit upon us all, and aid us in our work.' And you talk about it as though they had given you a shovel and told you to dig a hole. You speak of it as something to get over, elude, slide through.

"There, my friend, if all that is an insinuation, then I am guilty. But it is intended for plain speaking, in the hope that you won't make anything else out of it but just a lecture on the hideous carelessness, the unfaithfulness and disloyalty wihch you have just proposed to practice, and——"

"Just a minute. Let me into that lodge again, will you?" asked the New Brother.

"Sure, but what for?"

"So I can ask the Master for more committee work, because I believe I know how it ought to be done, and because I'm going to do it the right way," answered the New Brother.

"Are you insinuating you are going to work?" asked the Old Tiler, slyly.

"Not insinuating — I'm promising you!" answered the New Brother earnestly.

On Meaning in Words

"YOU know, I wonder why they don't revise the ritual. There is so much in it that is vague, obscure, and so many useless and unnecessary words and all; know what I mean? It would be so much clearer if—er— you know, if it were clearer."

"I suppose," the Old Tiler answered the New Brother, "that you think you could do a good job of revision?"

"You bet I could. Why, there are words there I never heard of until I became a Mason, and lots of places that the words could be changed and be more easily understood and read more like regular language, if you know what I mean."

"You don't seem to be able to say just what you mean," objected the Old Tiler. "Suppose you give me an instance."

"Well," said the New Brother, "let me see. Er—ah—well, I don't just remember exactly how it goes, but there is a place where it says, 'justice is that standard or boundary of right which enables us to render every man his just due without distinction.' Now, 'justice' isn't a standard or a boundary. It's a sentiment. It's just as true to say that 'right' is bounded by 'truth' or 'toleration' or 'mercy' as it is to say it is bounded by 'justice.' And to say that by justice we render men their just dues is like saying that by right we render men their right dues, and you can't explain a word with itself. If you understand what I mean——"

"Oh, I understand what I think you mean," answered the Old Tiler. "But I don't think you say what you mean. No one ever does say what they mean. No matter how carefully anyone tries, they say one thing and mean something else."

"Oh, nonsense. Why, everyone says what they mean when they stop to think about it."

"Is that so?" asked the Old Tiler, astonished. "Well, what do we have a Supreme Court for?"

"To interpret the laws; what's that got to do with it?"

"If the men who made the laws said what they meant, why do we have to have a Supreme Court to tell us what the men who framed the laws intended when they passed them? The Constitution of the United States is a plain and simple document, and yet someone is forever raising the question as to whether some law is constitutional or not. If I say to you, 'Boy, you are mistaken,' you think you know what I mean, but I haven't said it; I have said something else. I have called you 'boy' when I know you must be a man or you couldn't be a Mason and I have stated that you are mistaken, when what I really mean is that it is my opinion that you are mistaken, but that, having lived a long time I know quite well it may be I who am mistaken. You gather what I mean from custom, knowledge of men and my tone of voice; but you don't get my real meaning from what I say.

"At the peace conference a lot of men tried to say a lot of things and the whole world has spent all its time since trying to find out what they did mean. We write books about what it means. A political platform is supposed to be simple and understandable, but it never means what it says as we all find out the day after election.

"Now, you object to some words in the ritual. But I say you can't frame that sentence so it reads any more plainly; the meaning is there and you know the meaning when you hear it. If that is true, then it doesn't make any difference whether the words are the best words or not. Go read your Bible. I can find you 1,000 verses which don't say what they mean but the meaning of which you cannot mistake. 'Suffer little children to come unto me, for of such is the kingdom of heaven.' Do you think heaven is nothing but children? Do you think He wanted only small children and no big ones? Can they only get to heaven by coming to Him, and He dead to this earth 1,900 years? But you know what He meant when He said it; He meant that children were not to be kept from Him, and that the innocence and the sweetness and the beauty of childhood was 'of the kingdom of heaven.'

"Now, boy — I should say brother — if He spoke in parables and hidden meanings and found it better to address a world so they listened to the thought rather than the words, why should not Masonry do the same? And if you say, 'Well, but let's make it better now that we know,' I ask you if you think you could rewrite the Bible so that it was more beautiful. Personally, I think, 'In my Father's house are many mansions; if it were not so I would have told you,' is the most beautiful verse in the Bible, but that's a matter of taste. If you said, 'My Father has a house! It has many dwelling places in it. If the facts were otherwise I would have said so long ago.' Would you better His words? You certainly wouldn't better His meaning.

"Now, my son—I mean, my brother—the words of the ritual of Masonry may not always be the most aptly chosen, there may be many places where a doctor of philology and a competent searcher of the book of synonyms could make it seem plainer. But that any such changes and substitutions would make its meaning plainer, its truth plainer, its teachings plainer, I very much doubt."

"But it's so hard to memorize," protested the New Brother weakly.

"So is a piano hard to play but I never heard of a musician wanting to take off a few keys to make it easier," answered the Old Tiler. "Allow me to suggest that you go way back and sit down. Get me?"

"I understand what you mean, even if you don't say it," smiled the New Brother. "And you can go plumb to thunder!"

"You're quite welcome," answered the Old Tiler, taking the meaning and not the words to answer.

On Investigating a Petitioner

"I HAD a funny question asked me to-day," said the New Brother to the Old Tiler. "Chap who just got his Master Mason degree was assigned to his first committee on a petition. And he asked me, 'what do I do to find out about this fellow?' Wasn't that a bird of a question?"

"I should like to hear what sort of an animal your answer was," answered the Old Tiler. "So I ask you the same question. What do you do to find out about a petitioner when you are on his committee?"

"Oh, I take the duty very seriously, I assure you!" answered the New Brother. "I go and see him and find out if he has all his arms and legs and things; no maimed man is going to get in if I know it! I talk to him and size him up, and see what sort of a chap he is, and if I think he's all right I so report. If I have any cause to doubt anything, I talk to his employer."

"I thought so!" answered the Old Tiler. "You regard him as perfectly innocent until he is proved guilty, and satisfy yourself that he has two legs and arms. If he looks like a good fellow, you tell the lodge he is one, and I dare say if he has a dirty face and frayed pair of trousers you say he isn't ready to be a Master Mason!"

"Well, what's the matter with that? Isn't that what we are supposed to do?"

"Well, only partly," answered the Old Tiler. "Do you know Gus, of this lodge?"

"Everyone knows Gus! Chap who limps!"

"Well, do you think he is a good Mason?"

"As far as I can see he is, why?"

"Gus only has one leg, you know. Of course, he lost it after he became a Master Mason."

"Yes, I know. What's that got to do with it?"

"Only that it seems a proof that about the least important part of your duties is to find out whether a man has the correct number of members! I know it's law; we cannot admit the one-footed or the one-handed. Sometimes I think it a very cruel law. But it is the law. But when the law is stretched to say that a man with a finger or a toe missing, or one eye, or one ear, or a humped back, or a club foot, cannot become a Mason, then I know that there is a higher law than this one!"

"But leaving all that aside, it seems to me that your method of looking into the merits of an applicant leaves something to be desired. You say, 'If I think he's all right.' You haven't any business to think he's all right. You can't tell him from a criminal by sizing him up! You may be a remarkable judge of appearances, but the lodge doesn't appoint you on a petitioner's committee for your ability to 'size someone up.' It appoints you to go out and dig.

"You 'size a man up' by his appearance and by his speech. But many a good Mason has been made out of a man whose clothing was not fashionable and whose speech was rough. It is not the outward appearance which counts; it's the

Eighty-nine

man under the coat. And you can't discover the man under the coat just by looking at the coat.

"It's good American doctrine that a man is innocent until he is proved guilty, but that doctrine presupposes that some power has accused the man. The applicant for Masonic degrees is not accused of anything. He is in a position of asking a favor. Now, when a man comes and asks a favor it is his business to prove to you he is worthy of having that favor granted. You have every right to regard him as unfit for the favor until he is proved fit. You have every right to regard the applicant as not entitled to the degree of Master Mason until he shows you that he is fit.

"When I go after a petitioner to find out whether he is the kind of a man he ought to be to be a member of my lodge, I see him in his home. If he is married I want to see him with his wife. If he has a child or children, I want to see them. I want to see whether they hang around Daddy's neck or climb on his lap or cower away from him. I once went to see a man and waited for him, talking to his wife and children. They were a gay little pair and she a nice little woman. But they all three kept looking out the window anxiously. After a while mother saw the man coming. 'Hush, babies,' she said, 'be very quiet now, here comes Daddy.' And they hushed, indeed. The man didn't speak to them when he came in, and just nodded to his wife.

"I knew exactly the kind of man he was then. Oh, I didn't stop there. I gave him every chance. I went to his employers and talked with them, and with his fellow employes. And the net result was to discover an egotist, a self-seeker, a selfish and hard man, and I turned him down with joy that I had found out he wasn't of Masonic calibre.

"No man can pass me who cannot explain in words of one syllable why he wants to be a Mason. He has to argue that question out with me at length. And if I find it's because he thinks it will help him in business or because he thinks the lodge will take care of him or his if he loses his job, or because he is curious, he never gets in.

"I want to know of a man, does he pay his debts? If he is married, is he insured? If not, why not? If it's because he can't afford to be, then he can't afford to be a Mason. I would not willingly allow an uninsured married man to join my lodge, because he hasn't the first conception of the protection of dependent loved ones, which marks a man as a man. I won't let a man pass who isn't trusted by his fellows; and I have let a man pass me who wouldn't be able to get in a business man's club or a fashionable church.

"It's the man inside, not the outside man, which counts."

"I think I better go hunt up the chap who asked me what I thought was a funny question and give him a better answer!" said the New Brother. "I—I didn't think there was all that in it."

"You just didn't think!" answered the Old Tiler.

"No, I didn't. But I'm right pleased with this conversation," added the New Brother.

"How so?" asked the Old Tiler.

"Because I remember you were on my committee!"

On Spending Money "Foolishly"

"IT'S a funny thing to me," said the New Brother, "why Masons spend their money so foolishly!"

"A fool and his money are soon parted," agreed the Old Tiler.

"Why, do you think Masons are fools?"

"Certainly not. I was just agreeing with you that when Masons spend money foolishly they were foolish. What particular variety of foolish spending is teasing you just now?"

"Oh, a lot of things. Here we go, spending $5 to send a funeral wreath to every brother's funeral, and $3 for flowers every time a brother is sick, and $2 for fruit every time he goes to a hospital. We spend money for decorating the lodge room when we have an entertainment. We spend money for food to feed men who are well fed at home. We spend money to hire entertainers when we have a blow-out and we are forever and always building a temple somewhere which costs a lot of money. My idea would be to put all that money in an educational fund or a charity fund or——"

"Do you, by any chance," interrupted the Old Tiler, "figure that you are delivering a lecture? Because I want to talk, too!"

"And I want you to talk. Tell me that I am right and that we do spend our money foolishly!"

"I can't do that," answered the Old Tiler. "But perhaps I can show you that we have something to say on our side. Let me take up your complaints in order. You object to $5 funeral wreaths to deceased brethren, and would rather see the money put in charity. Did you suppose we send the wreath to comfort the dead man? He is beyond our help. We send it to offer what consolation there is to the family in the thought that we, his brethren, care that he has died. We send it that the world may see that we hold our deceased brother in honor. If we are careless of grief when grief comes to the loved ones of those we love, the world will hold it against us, and our influence be lessened.

"We send the flowers to the sick and the fruit to the hospital, that the ill brother may have that cheering spiritual comfort of knowing that in his hour of need his brethren forget him not. Is there any prettier charity than that? Is it, in your mind, more charitable to feed a hungry body than a hungry heart? Have you ever been ill in a hospital? Did no one remember you with a cheery card, a flower, a basket of fruit? If you were unremembered, you passed a sad hour in the thought that no one cared. If friends brought their friendship before you when you needed it most, you were helped on your way to recovery . . . and if we hold not our hand beneath to cheer and help a worthy brother, for what, I ask you, does our brotherhood stand?

"Why should we not decorate a lodge room for an entertainment? Do you, in your home, live in bare walls, without pictures, carpets or pretty furniture? Do you take all you make over a bare subsistence and give to the poor? Do the poor themselves spend their all only in food? Or will you, in a poor man's home, find a flower, a book, a picture? Beauty is as much a need of life as food. Cows chew their cud contentedly in barn or field, but man must chew the cud of life with a spiritual as well as a physical outlook, and beauty is as necessary for that as bread. The lodge room is our home. To decorate it for entertainment is merely that men remember their Masonic home as beautiful with the thought of pleasures taken together . No, I cannot call that a waste of money.

"And the same applies when we hire others to entertain us. Refreshment, whether in the form of sandwiches and coffee or a vocal or instrumental solo, refreshes mind and body; one or the other, or both, are better for having eaten and drunk with other bodies also eating or drinking. The solo we listen to alone gives us not half the pleasure which comes from listening to one in company. The few cents per capita we spend for our refreshment is no more money wasted than were the 10 cents you paid for your cigar or the 15 cents for which you had your shoes shined!

"As for the temples we build, for what could we spend our money better? Charity, indeed, is good, but charity which spends one's all impoverishes both the giver and the recipient. If Masonry is a power in the world it is because it ensnares men's hearts. But men are but children grown, and they see through children's eyes. To the childish eye the great temple means a great fraternity. Our religion is founded in a great temple. Beautiful churches erected to the honor of the Father are not thought to distract from the principles of charity His religion teaches. Why should not we erect a great temple to that philosophy which is founded on a belief in and honor of, the Great Architect of the Universe?

"Suppose the whole world spent no money except for food, clothes and charity? The poor would become rich, and the virtues of ambition, thrift, independence and manhood would become extinct. If there were no music, painting, love of flowers, beautiful buildings, in the world, where would our hearts reach when they fling tendrils out seeking to touch something they know is just beyond? We do not see God in the ham sandwich as we do in the beautiful notes of music; I'll agree He is everywhere, but we find Him easiest through our love and appreciation of the lovely, rather than the mundane things of life.

"Would you cease printing Bibles that more hungry people could be fed? Logically, you think that no money not spent for charity is money well spent, but I say to you that charity is but a part of Masonry. Masonry teaches men to help themselves. It teaches men to think. It teaches men to aid their fellows, not only by the charity gift, but by the spiritual gift of encouragement, cheer, help, aid, love, the kindly word. And when we can express them, or any other Masonic virtue, in the flower, the basket of fruit, the song, the little refreshment or the great and beautiful temple, then I say we spend our money wisely.

"Truly the fool and his money are soon parted, but the fool parts with his for foolishness, and we part with ours for value received, pressed

Ninety-five

down and running over to carry Masonic cheer to the hearts of our brethren, sick or well."

"Of course you are right, as you always are," agreed the New Brother. "By the way, you are the chairman of the committee on hospitals, are you not? Stick that in your pocket and make the next bunch of flowers or basket of fruit twice as big."

The "that" with which the New Brother soothed his conscience was green and crinkled as it was folded.

On the Painful Process of Becoming a Past Master

THE newly elected and installed Master had finished his speech. In it he had promised many things to the lodge, and outlined a beautiful program for the coming year. In conclusion he said: "Thus I hope to make my year a good year. I propose to increase the attendance, better the degree work, have more entertainment, see that instruction is more carefully carried on, do more charity, have better turnouts at such funerals as we may have to hold; in other words, with your assistance, I propose to make this the most attractive lodge in the world."

"Pretty nice speech," said the New Brother, sitting down beside the Old Tiler. "You know, I think I'd like to go in line."

"Indeed, it was a very good speech. The boy has the makings of a real Past Master," smiled the Old Tiler. "But about going in line—don't forget the process hurts."

"Hurts? I don't believe I get you exactly."

"Probably not. When you have been longer in the lodge, you will recognize a certain similarity about all speeches from newly elected and installed Masters. They all think the same way. As soon as they get near the east they begin to think what they can do for the lodge and how they can make it better. They make high plans and do a lot of brain work, and then they tell the lodge about it. I wonder it never occurs to any of them how conceited they are when they are first elected."

"Conceited? Why, young Jamison isn't conceited; he's a nice, modest chap."

"Sure he is! But he tells you all the things he is going to do, quite forgetting that a long line of predecessors have not succeeded in doing them. They talk that way with the world and the lodge at their feet, and both to be conquered.

"But neither ever is conquered. Every Past Master has done all he knew to make this the best lodge in the world. It's a pretty good lodge at that, but it isn't what it might be—if we were all perfect. As any Master's year slips along and he finds that the attendance isn't much better than it was, and the degree work just as lacking in beauty as it had ever been because this, that, and the other officer, with the best intentions but no equipment, is making a spectacle of himself, he finds that the process of becoming a Past Master hurts, and hurts badly.

"Most Past Masters are worth a lot more to the lodge as Past Masters than as Masters because of the lessons they learn while Master which they didn't know before. And Jamison has the makings of a fine Past Master; one who will think and work, and be a genuine asset to the lodge."

"But Jamison will improve the degree work— he has a lot of plans——"

"He'll try. But, my brother, you can't make men over. All our officers are pretty fixed in their ways. They do the best that is in them to do. They are earnest, lovable, conscientious men. They struggle to learn the work, letter perfect.

But God makes some men orators, and to some he gives a sing-song voice which would ruin the most beautiful words in the language; and we have our share of them. Jamison won't be able to change them, hard as he may try."

"Do you think he shouldn't try, then?"

"Heaven forbid! Of course he should try. We should all try. The officers should try, and do try. But if we all succeeded in our straining after perfection, there wouldn't be any fun left in the world at all, or any glory in Masonry. In a perfect world Masonry would have no place. Since Masonry is in existence to make men better, if all men were best it wouldn't be needed.

"No, Brother, it's a good thing for the lodge that Jamison can't make this a perfect lodge of perfect Masons. If he could, we wouldn't have any excuse for being. But if he didn't try, he wouldn't be the good man that he is."

"Well, I am amazed," said the New Brother. "You have such peculiar ideas——"

"I am an old, old tiler," grinned the Old Tiler. "I have watched them go up to the east with high hopes and great plans for years and years. And I have seen them step down at the end of their year, happy to be out of the chair, deeply sorry they couldn't do what they tried to do, disillusioned as to the capacity of one man to change a thousand men, worried that they haven't carried the old lodge farther on the road.

"But years have taught me that it is given to very few of us to set many stones in the structure of Masonry. We are lucky if we set one brick right—if, indeed, we can bring one stone which is good work, true work, square work, to the structure, and receive therefor a Mason's wages, we have done well.

"And that is what Jamison will do. He won't succeed in making fifty more men come to the lodge this year than came last. He won't stage a degree any better than a dozen Masters before him have staged. He won't have any more calls for charity than many have had. He won't have any better candidates or any better taught entered apprentices or fellowcrafts than others have had. He will just go along with the lodge, and guide it and direct it and do the best he can, but, unless he is the one man in a hundred, he won't do any more than all of them who trod that road before him could do."

"Then you think he'll be a failure?"

"Decidedly not! I think he'll be a success. For he will try: try earnestly, try hard, think, labor and struggle with his job. And at the end of a year he will have set one stone in this lodge, at much cost to himself. He will make himself into a good Past Master, a man who knows his lodge, who understands its membership, who is able to think fast and work hard, a man who loves his order and his jewel. The one thing he can do best for this lodge is to make himself into a good Past Master—and if he does that, he will find, in after years, that it paid, even if it did hurt."

"I—I don't know that I want to go in line," said the New Brother, thoughtfully, as he walked away.

On a Lodge Budget

"IT is an outrage, a shame, a disgrace! That committee ought to be indicted for defaming the fair fame of Masonry!" The New Brother was indignantly emphatic.

"It sounds perfectly terrible to me," agreed the Old Tiler, sympathetically; "what was the committee and what did it do?"

"Why, that Committee on the Budget. And they brought in a report which is to lie over for a month before discussion, and I am just seething with indignation!"

"Well, seethe out loud a bit. Maybe I can seethe, too, and there will be two of us doing it!" suggested the Old Tiler without a smile.

"Oh, you'll seethe all right!" assured the New Brother. "The committee has averaged our income from past years to find what we can get this year. Then they have laid aside a fund of $2,000, subtracted the fixed charges from what is left, and apportioned the remainder among our other activities."

"Well, isn't that all right?" asked the Old Tiler.

"You don't understand! This committee has dared to say that we should spend only so much for entertainment, only so much for relief and charity, only so much for education!"

"I guess I am getting old or stupid or something," said the Old Tiler. "That sounds perfectly reasonable to me!"

"What? Reasonable to decide beforehand that we can't spend but a certain amount in a year for charity? For entertainment? For education? Why, Masonry is built on the thought of relief! How can we function as Masons should if we are to circumscribe our charities?"

"Softly, softly!" countered the Old Tiler. "Perhaps, in your excitement, you forget that Masonry is founded not only on relief but on brotherly love and truth as well. And if we spend all our resources on relief, where do we get the money to spend on 'truth' and on cementing the ties of 'brotherly love'?"

"Oh, fine words!" cried the New Brother. "But this report puts it down in figures, and says that only such and such a percentage of our receipts must be spent in charity and——"

"Now, wait a minute!" The Old Tiler roused himself and spoke sharply for the first time. "Either you didn't listen to the report or you couldn't understand it. Evidently you didn't know that they did me the honor to make me a member of that Budget Committee, so I know all about it. The Budget Committee didn't say one word in its report about confining charity to the amount stated. It merely said that the average expended for charity during the past five years was so-and-so much, so that we could reasonably look forward to spending a similar amount in the coming year. The figure was set down in order to allow a basis of comparison and a decision as to how much could be spent for other purposes.

"Running a lodge without a budget is as foolish as trying to run an automobile without gasoline. The budget is the instrument by which we determine how and where and when and why we are to function. Without a budget we over-play our hand. Without a budget we are apt to spend too much in entertainment and not enough in relief. Without a budget we may put ourselves in the position of robbing our future brethren by encroaching upon the capital assets of the lodge. With a budget we have an adviser constantly at our elbow saying, 'go slow, Brother,' when we start to splurge on something which, no matter how worthy, may be beyond our means."

"That sounds very nice," said the New Brother, a little less excitedly, "but you still don't explain what we are going to do when our charity calls exceed the average of the past five years."

"Do? Why, we are going to meet them, of course," snapped the Old Tiler. "No Masonic lodge ever ducked a call for charity when it had the means or the credit. But if we find that the fund for charity is twice as big as we expected, then we know we must cut down on the entertainment. If we have no budget and no line to which to hew, we go on the same old way, spending just as much for entertainment as before, and so coming out at the end of the year a loser."

"But this budget cut down on a lot of things; we have to use less printed matter or cheaper printed matter, and we are only allowed a certain sum for ladies' night instead of——"

"Instead of giving a committee of three authority to loot the lodge treasury of all that's in it to provide free entertainment for a lot of fellows to give their wives and sweethearts! You said it!

And while no man in this lodge loves his wife any better than I love mine, I am perfectly willing to stand up in meeting and say that I am content to have the lodge entertain her once a year with a sandwich and a cup of coffee, and undertake her entertainment on more elaborate lines myself. Don't forget, my brother, that our primary purpose is neither charity nor entertainment, and that when we make either or both the principal parts of our Masonic activities, we are actually working against the best interests of the fraternity rather than for them.

"Masonry is a cultivation of love between man and man; it is education, as between heart and heart. It stands for patriotism, for freedom of thought and conscience, for a simple devoutness, for reverence, as well as for fun and frolic. Our ancient brethren found 'refreshment' necessary, but only when the 'work' was done; the 'pay as you please' system of too many lodges always skimps something, and it's usually the work, not the refreshment. No, Brother, I'm for the budget, and for it strong."

"So am I!" agreed the New Brother, in a very small voice.

On Masonic Talk

"I'M seeking a little light," said the New Brother, sitting down by the Old Tiler and proffering his cigar case.

"I think I have a match——," the Old Tiler felt in his pocket.

"I get you, Steve!" grinned the New Brother, "but that's not the kind of light I am looking for. I want Masonic light, or at least, light on a Masonic subject."

"Well, I don't pretend to be the great and only Masonic illuminant," said the Old Tiler, slowly, "but if I have what you want, be sure I'll let it shine."

"Well, it's this," began the New Brother. "Every now and then I find a certain amount of Masonic talk going on in public places. For instance, there was a poker game going on in a smoking room of a club where I was the other night, and I heard one say, rather cleverly, 'Them you have passed, but me I shall not pass. I open ——.' You hear lots of men say they will do this or that on the square or on the level. I run across 'and govern yourself accordingly' in print every now and then. I want to know whether such public quotations from Masonic work are against good Masonic practice?"

"Well, now," answered the Old Tiler, "it seems to me your question isn't very complete. It doesn't mean much of anything."

"Why not?"

"Well, it doesn't take any account of motives. If you hear a man say that the stream rose and his house and his children were in danger, but that Providence dropped a tree across the rushing waters, and that in His mercy God damned the stream, you are certain you have heard testimony to His glory. And if you hear some man in the street couple the name of Deity with the word which begins with D, you know you listen to profanity. Same sounds in each case; difference is, the motive, the meaning.

"So, if I tell a man that I will do what I say I will do 'on the square,' he understands that I mean rightly, well, honestly, uprightly. If then he also gathers that the expression is a Masonic one, surely the fraternity has not been injured by my use of the words. But if I say to a stranger, or within a stranger's hearing, 'these are certain Masonic words, and we use them in the degrees,' and then I repeat various phrases, why then I am skirting dangerously close to breaking my obligation, and, by the very fact that I seem to be careless with my order's business, I am doing that order harm!"

"I see!" said the New Brother. "That's very plain. But how about when a fellow wants to find out if you are a Mason? Suppose I meet a man on a train with a Masonic pin on, and I am not satisfied and want to examine him Masonically. What about that?"

"You shouldn't ever want to do things which can't be done, my son!" laughed the Old Tiler. "You might, indeed, put the stranger through an examination as to what Masonry he knew, but it wouldn't be Masonic. You have no right to constitute yourself an examining committee. That is lodge business."

"But suppose he wants to talk Masonic secrets with me?"

"My brother, no Mason ever wants to talk Masonic secrets with any man he doesn't know to be a Mason! You can be sure that the man who wants to talk secrets with you, without having sat in lodge with you, or being vouched for to you, is either a very new or a very poor Mason or no Mason at all!"

"But surely one can talk Masonry with strangers; if they wear the pin and have a card they are probably Masons, and——"

"Surely. Talk all the Masonry you want to! But make sure it is the sort of Masonic talk you could utter in the presence of your wife, or a priest. Your true Mason won't want you to talk any other kind in public. Not very long ago I was on a train, and behind me two men, neither of them Masons, got to arguing about Masonry. The things those men knew which were not so were something wonderful! But I never opened my mouth. And the conductor, whom I have known for years as a Mason, heard them, and all he did was wink a wunk at me. We knew the truth; they didn't. What was the use of stirring up an argument?"

"Well, how about giving some sign or word in a mixed company, so I can let the other fellows know I am a Mason?" asked the New Brother.

"Oh!" cried the Old Tiler. "You've been reading novels! You have an idea when you go to a card party you ought to wiggle your ears or some-

One hundred seven

thing, so the other Masons will know you are one, too! Nothing to that, my son. Masonic recognitions are not for pleasure, but for need; they are not for show, but for use. You have been taught how to let others know, if you need to. You know how to recognize a Mason when he lets you know. But these things are not for social gatherings, and the man who lards his speech with Masonic expressions merely to show off— well, he's like the man who uses Deity and that other word together when he isn't testifying to the goodness of the Creator; his motive is wrong!"

"Well, I asked for light, and I received it. I am not sure but what we could substitute you for one of the Lesser Lights," said the New Brother.

"If you mean that for a joke," said the Old Tiler slowly, "I shall think my words were wasted on you."

"I didn't," protested the New Brother. "I was only trying to say, perhaps clumsily, that I thought you'd make a good Master!"

"Then I shall think only of the motive, thank you for the compliment, and forget the way you put it!" smiled the Old Tiler.

On Outside Activities

"WELL, it seems to me we are coming to a pretty pass in our Masonry!" said the New Brother, disgustedly.

"That has a familiar ring! No times like the old times, no days like the old days, everything going to the demnition bow-wows— seems to me they have uncovered inscriptions that read like that in King Tut's tomb!" grinned the Old Tiler. "What's wrong with our Masonry now?"

"Why, all these extras we are collecting in the lodge. First, we have a choir; that's all right, since music adds to the solemnity and beauty of the degrees. But now we are getting up a lodge glee club. There is a saxophone quartet being formed, and there is talk of a lodge band. There's a brother in there to-night who has been in lodge long enough to know better, organizing a lodge dramatic society. If he has any dramatic instinct I should think he'd put it into the degrees. The Master is trying to interest some brethren in forming a new Masonic club, and a lot of brethren are talking of a camping club, for summer fishing! I think it's a shame, this scattering of effort; we ought to put it all into the work of the lodge; don't you agree with me?"

"I sure do; I think all our effort Masonic should be Masonic effort!" answered the Old Tiler.

"There! I think that's the first time I ever started a discussion with you and found you were on my side!" laughed the New Brother, triumphantly.

"Well," said the Old Tiler, judicially, "I wouldn't go as far as to say I was on your side of the fence this time. I agree our efforts ought to be Masonic, but I don't see anything but Masonic effort in a lodge glee club, saxophone quartet club, camping association, dramatic club, and so on. What's wrong with them as Masonic work?"

"Why, Masonic work is putting on the degrees well, and making an impression on the candidate and charity, and—and——"

"Go on, Son, you are doing fine!"

"Oh, you know what I mean! Masonic work isn't going camping or playing a saxophone!"

"Isn't it?" asked the Old Tiler, interestedly. "Now, that's a plain statement of what you believe to be a fact, and I can argue with you from now until to-morrow morning! But you must explain why playing a saxophone in a lodge for the pleasure of the lodge isn't Masonic."

"Oh, the time spent could be better spent in—in listening to the degrees."

"Granted, if there were degrees to listen to. But you wouldn't have us put on degree without reason? If you find the lodge neglecting its degree work to listen to a quartet, I'll agree the quartet does harm. But if you find the quartet bringing down a lot of brethren who like music, and to whom we can then give Masonic instruction, I can't agree that it isn't good Masonic work."

"Well, how about the dramatic club and the fishing association?"

"Why," answered the Old Tiler, "I think they are the same in intent. The dramatic club will gather together a lot of brethren from the lodge interested in dramatics. It will develop histrionic talent which now doesn't exist. It will train men to do good, sincere, and well-managed Masonic degree work. But if it never led a single man into our degree teams, it would still be a bond of union between a lot of men who would thus get better acquainted among themselves, and the better lodge members know each other the more united the lodge and the better Masonic work it can do.

"The same thing applies to a fishing club. Fishing is an innocent and delightful sport. When Masons congregate together to enjoy an innocent and delightful sport, and prefer the company of each other to the company of a mixed club, it, to my mind, speaks very highly of the bonds of brotherhood by which they are knit. It is an attractive idea to me, and if I can afford it I will surely join. I'd much rather be able to tell some fish that he has passed all the other anglers, but me he cannot pass, in the presence of my brethren than have to keep my thoughts to myself in the presence of a lot of strangers!"

"You think, then, that all these extra growths on the body of the lodge don't sap its strength as a lodge?"

"I don't think they are growths on the body of the lodge at all! I think you make your mistake in supposing that brethren who do these things are taking strength from the lodge. I think their banding together to sing, to play musical instruments, to fish, to act in plays together, shows that they have a real feeling of brotherhood. I think the more such activities we can engage in the more united a band we will be. And I know, from as many years in the fraternity as you have put in weeks, my brother, that the more united we are, the more good men we attract, the greater pride we have in our work, and therefore the better and more educational is the strictly Masonic, or degree work, which we do.

"All work and no play makes a Mason a stay-at-home. Our ancient brethren specified the usages of refreshment. They understood that playing together was as necessary as working together. If part of us can play together for our own pleasure, well and good. If part of us can play together for our own pleasure and at the same time give pleasure to others, well and better. And if we can pleasure ourselves, please others, and at the same time benefit the lodge by increasing its unity, why, well and best of all!"

"Dog-gone it all, you sure are a salesman!" said the New Brother. "I ought not to afford it, but——"

"Why, what have I sold you?" asked the Old Tiler, interestedly.

"Memberships in the glee club, the Masonic club, and the fishing club!" snapped the New Brother, but he grinned as he spoke.

On Substitutes at Funerals

"DARN it" said the New Member, "I got drawn on a funeral committee. And of course they have to hold it on the very day and at the very hour I want to play golf. I wonder if I can find a substitute?"

"Very likely," answered the Old Tyler. "The world is full of substitutes who do the work and perform the duties of people too lazy, too inefficient, too careless of the rights of others to do it themselves."

"Oh, come now, don't be so rough," said the New Member, wincing. "You know and I know that this going to funerals is all form. Why, I never saw this deceased brother, to my knowledge. What earthly difference will it make to him or his family if I go to his funeral myself or get someone else to go for me?"

"No difference at all," agreed the Old Tyler. "The only person it will make any difference to will be you."

"The difference it will make to me will be the difference between being bored and having a good game of golf," asserted the New Brother.

"Oh, yes, it will make other differences," the Old Tiler was very emphatic. "Son, let me tell you a few things you apparently don't know. One of them is that the only importance Masonry has is what it does to a man's heart. Objectively, it is of less importance than the necktie he wears. The important part of Masonry is its leavening power on that part of a man which is the ego, the person, the individual.

"Now, that effect which Masonry has on a man's heart is aided by what I might call the mechanics of Masonry, the temple, the lodge room, the dignity of the order, its public appearances, the respect it shows to its dead, its charity, its educational work, its appeal to the general public, its secrecy, its reputation of being above party and politics, its alliance with all religion and its participation in none. These things make Masonry objective, but they are but the outward semblance of the inward and spiritual part of Masonry. These inward spiritual parts you ought to know for yourself: charity, relief, brotherly love, truth, knowledge, self-sacrifice, toleration.

"But how can you separate the inward and spiritual from the outward and objective? You can't! We build beautiful temples and meet in beautiful churches, to express our love for our belief. We try to have lodge work dignified, well done, impressive, to express to ourselves our sense of the beauty and dignity of the spiritual truths we teach. And we go to and conduct the funeral of a deceased brother, not to make a show before the world, not to appear in public, not to be a part of a parade of grief, but in order to express to ourselves our sincere feeling of regret that one we loved as a brother has departed and our honest conviction that he has but traveled onward and upward to that Temple Not Made With

Hands, where the Supreme Architect waits for all who, Masons and profane alike, have been builders upon earth.

"It is true that the world does judge by externals. As we make an impressive appearance at a funeral, so do the profane judge us. As we make a poor and straggling appearance at a funeral, we are judged by those who do not know Masonry from the inside. Therefore it is important to us who have a care for the good name of Masonry in the world at large that our funerals shall be well attended and that we conform to these outward marks of grief which custom has determined to be essential at a funeral.

"In order to make a good appearance at a funeral it is usual to have a funeral committee. In large lodges it is much more essential than in small, because in small lodges everyone knows everyone else and goes to a funeral because he wants to. In large lodges we don't know everyone, and unless we have a committee we don't put up the right kind of a 'front' at a funeral. The more obscure and unknown the brother the less the size of the lodge turnout. Hence the committee, chosen by lot or alphabetical order.

"In this lodge we have nearly 1,000 members and we chose fifty brethren by the alphabet. Once in twenty funerals then, your name will be drawn. If we have five funerals a year, which is an average, you will be called upon once in four years to aid your lodge to show its respect for the real grief of the family of a departed brother, and to express to the profane the thought that Masonry honors its own.

One hundred fifteen

"You can get a substitute. I will substitute for you if you wish. I have no golf game to attract me. I substitute for a good many men and I never refuse if I can help it. Sometimes I substitute because of a real reason; business, absence, illness. Sometimes I substitute because a man is too careless and too lazy to do his own work. But if he is too lazy and too careless, nothing I can do will help him. For the sake of the lodge I go in his place. For his own sake I try to show him first, what a mistake he makes in delegating to another the duty he owes his fraternity.

"But I never feel I am doing too much when I am drawn or when I substitute. Masonry means something in my heart. I know it means more as its reputation is good and grows. If anything I can do, no matter how little, aids that reputation, I am glad to do it. When is this funeral you want me to attend for you?"

"I don't want you to," answered the New Member. "I got to go now——"

"What's your hurry?" asked the Old Tyler.

"I want to see the Master or the secretary and tell him to put me down as a possible substitute next time, when someone does what I was going to do and now am never going to do—miss my chance to do my last duty to one of my brethren."

"Umph!" said the Old Tiler.

On All Kinds of Masonry

"WELL," said the New Brother, as he displayed a sheaf of cards to the Old Tiler, "I am almost through. Pretty soon I will have joined them all and become every kind of a Mason there is."

"Why, what do you know about the kinds of Masons there are?" asked the Old Tiler, interestedly. "You have hardly been a Master Mason long enough to gain all that knowledge!"

"Why, I don't think that's hard to gain; not with all the brethren poking petitions at you. There are Scottish Rite Masons and York Rite Masons and Templar Masons and Chapter Masons and Council Masons and——"

"Oh!" The syllable said much. Then the Old Tiler added, "I didn't understand. I thought you couldn't have learned yet."

"Learned what? Are there some more kinds of Masons?"

"Indeed, yes!" answered the Old Tiler. "A great many kinds. But there are six kinds you haven't mentioned at all, which stand out more prominently than many others."

"Do tell me. I thought I had joined most of them——"

"You don't join these. You become one of them, or are made one of them, or grow into one of them. For instance, there is the King Solomon Mason. He thinks that everything that Solomon did as a Mason is right and everything that he didn't do is wrong. To him Masonry was conceived, born and grew up in the shadow of King Solomon, and every word in it is literally true. He is like the man who believes so literally in the Bible that he refuses to believe the earth is round, because there is a verse in the Bible which refers to the 'four corners of the earth!' The King Solomon Mason is the literal-minded cuss and lives his Masonry according to his light: perhaps it's not his fault it is so dim.

"Then there is the ritual Mason. To him the importance of Masonry is the form of its words. He is a good Mason, in this man's mind, if he can repeat a lecture from end to end without a slip; a man may do battle, murder, or cause sudden death, commit arson or run away with his neighbor's wife; if he knows the ritual, it 'was all a mistake.' The man who doesn't know his ritual letter perfect is not, in this man's eyes, a good Mason; not though he give to charity with both hands and carry love for his fellowman in both head and heart.

"The practical Mason is the Mason who looks at everything from a utilitarian standpoint. He prefers electricity to candles for Lesser Lights because they are simpler and prefers candles to electricity because they are cheaper. He thinks a choir impractical because it doesn't produce anything permanent, and would rather spend the money for printed matter or a new carpet. He is at his best when raising money for a new temple and at his worst when asked to express himself upon the spirit of Masonry. His hand is in his pocket for charity, but never for entertainment.

One hundred eighteen

He is always on the finance committee, and usually recommends a budget in which rent and heat and light are bigger than relief or charity.

"The heart Mason is the exact opposite. Masonry with the heart Mason is not practical; it is visionary. He is full of impractical schemes. He is always starting a new temple which will never be built, and talks much of the Fatherhood of God and the Brotherhood of Man, but is conspicuously absent when the hat is passed and the committee on funds needs a few workers to go out and gather in. The heart Mason is the lodge sob sister; he always seconds any motion to spend any amount of money for flowers or sending a brother away for his health, and always makes a hectic little tear-filled speech about the fatherless loved ones, even if the dear departed died a bachelor.

"The business Mason belongs because it helps his job. He is always sitting next to the solid business men and likes to tell people what his job is. If he is a Past Master, he absolutely never comes to lodge on time; that is so he can get a special welcome at the altar. His favorite speech is about the man who tried to advertise his business in lodge and how evil this was; in the speech he always mentions his own business. He wears an extra large sized pin and prints squares and compasses on his letterheads.

"You will need no explanation of that miscalled member whom we denominate by the rather crude but expressive term of belly Mason. He is the chap who is most faithful in attendance at other lodges where there may be a feed. He will cheerfully spend 20 cents car fare and a long evening to get a 10-cent sandwich. If there is to be a regular sit-down feed he will sit up all night to be on time. If the affair is in another lodge and needs tickets he will take days off from his job to hunt a brother who has a ticket and doesn't want it. He usually manages to cross the lodge room while the cigars are passed so he can dig into the box twice. If the crowd is small, he is the last man to get a smoke, so he can take all that are left. If the crowd is large, he is among the first, to make sure he doesn't get left.

"And then there is the regular Mason—the fellow who does his best with the time and brains he has. He is the great bulk of the fraternity. He it is who pays the dues and fills the chairs and does the work. He is seldom a fine ritualist, but he is usually an earnest one. He is not very practical, and would spend more than we have if it wasn't that he is too sentimental to permit that charity fund to be robbed. He passes the sandwiches and coffee, and if there is any left he likes his, but he doesn't care so long as the evening is a success. He isn't a student, but something deep down in the heart of Masonry has reached deep down into his heart, and so he comes to lodge and does his best. He is not learned, but he is not stupid. He is not hidebound, and yet he is conservative. He loves his lodge, but not so much he cannot see her faults. He is most of us."

"And what class Mason am I?" asked the New Brother, uneasily looking at his sheaf of cards.

"Well," answered the Old Tiler, "you have cards enough to be considered a Mason for almost any reason, but I'll take your word for it; what kind of a Mason are you?"

"I don't know for sure, but I know now what kinds I am never going to be!" answered the New Brother, putting his many cards away.

On Subscribing for a Temple

"I DON'T hold with this subscription idea at all," announced the New Brother to the Old Tiler. "My idea of Masonry is that it should be a self-supporting institution and not ask for contributions."

"Yes, yes, go on, you interest me. So does the braying of a jackass and the gurgling of a six months old child interest me, also the bleating of a lamb and the raucous cries of the crow."

"Well, you can call it that if you like," defended the New Brother, "but this idea of asking for contributions to build a temple is all wrong."

"Suppose you tell me what you mean when you say that Masonry ought to be self supporting," suggested the Old Tiler.

"Why, it ought to get along on its dues and fees."

"Oh, then you think you ought to get along entirely on your salary. You don't think you should borrow money from the bank to build a house, or to aid you in the prosecution of your business?"

"Why not? That's different."

"How is it different? You borrow to build a house, and the house is security for the loan. Some day you pay it back and own the house. We borrow from our members to build a temple and——"

"But that's just the point. We don't borrow, we beg. And in the future we don't pay back, we just grab the temple and the fellows that have paid for it have nothing to show for it."

"Well, now let's see," answered the Old Tiler. "Suppose we 'beg' as you put it, sufficient contributions from our membership to build the temple and own it outright. The only money we then have to spend on it is upkeep, overhead. We won't have to charge ourselves rent for it, because we won't be paying on a loan. In our present temple we are, and so we pay rent. The lodges pay that rent. If they have no rent to pay they will have so much more in the treasury. When a lodge has more than it needs in the treasury it may either reduce its dues or spend more in charity or entertainment. The mere reducing of the rent charge will soon equal, per capita, the entire contribution asked of any individual brother.

"But quite apart from the mere dollars and cents angle, did you ever consider that a temple of Masonry is much more than a mere pile of stone, in which are rooms where Masons may meet? The temple expresses Masonry to all the world. As it is beautiful, solid, substantial, massive, permanent, so does the fraternity appear to the world. As it is paid for, free from debt, a complete asset, so does the institution seem to be, to the profane. A poor, mean temple argues lodge members with so little belief in their order that they are not willing to provide it with proper quarters. Just as a beautiful church expresses love and veneration for the Creator, by those who build it, so does a beautiful building for Masonry express love and veneration for the order

One hundred twenty-three

and reverence for the Great Architect in Whose shadow we labor and to Whom all temples of Masonry are erected, call Him by what name we will.

"The brethren here have undertaken to erect a beautiful temple. They want to have, first, a meeting place which is convenient and comfortable, one in which they can take proper pride and through which they can show visitors that Masonry, here, as elsewhere, has love for its tenets. But they want also to express to the world the feeling they have for the most wonderful vision of true brotherhood ever given to man. So they say to each other, 'Brother, how much will you give?' and brother answers brother, 'All I can afford,' and does so.

"Now suppose we had done this differently. Suppose we had assessed each lodge so much; the lodges would have been impoverished and the members enriched not at all. We are not asking any great amount from each member; less than $2 a month, less than ten cents a day. But it is enough so that each brother, as he gives, will feel that he is really making some little sacrifice for the order he loves. When the temple is built every brother who contributed will feel that it is truly his temple, his in the actual sense of intimate personal ownership. He may look at a block of stone in the wall and say to himself, 'That is mine; I paid for it.' And what a man has bought, because he loved it, he cherishes. Nothing which this jurisdiction could do would more thoroughly solidify Masonry than this universal appeal, this universal response. When we have it finished, it will be our temple in the truest sense of the term; ours not only that we went down in our pockets and paid for it, but ours because we have put our hearts into it. And what a man puts his heart in, that he cherishes, defends, upholds, makes better.

"We are spending $100 a brother, perhaps, and we are giving every brother $1,000 worth of pride of ownership, of love for his order. We are building not only for the brethren who are here and who should shoulder the burden in the heat of the day, but for the brethren who come after.

"Our ancient brethren who built the great temples of the middle ages for all to see and revere have left their mark on time and history and on generations of men who have followed them. We will leave our mark on generations of our sons and their sons and their sons' sons after them, all because we have been willing to go down in our pockets and make a free will offering to that thing, which next to God, is the greatest leaven of our life, the fraternity which makes a man love his fellow men."

"Oh, darn it, stop talking. Twice while you have been lecturing me I have mentally increased my subscription. Now I have doubled it. Hush, or I wont be able to buy shoes for the baby."

"Well, don't start things, then!" grumbled the Old Tiler, but he smiled as he held out a fresh subscription blank and a fountain pen.

On Entertainment and Ladies' Nights

"IT'S perfectly disgusting to me," said the New Brother. "I think old Morton must think a lot more of his stomach than he does of his Masonry. Insisting on expensive refreshments for ladies' night. And I don't see what's the use of a ladies' night, anyhow. Tom Jenkins is trying to start a ball game and Elliot Jones wants a picnic; what's the matter with these chaps, anyway? All this isn't Masonry!"

"No?" asked the Old Tiler. "Why isn't it?"

"Why, what a foolish question. You know what Masonry is. You know it isn't just enjoyment and foolishness."

"Well, I've been in Masonry thirty-seven years," said the Old Tiler, "and maybe I know what it is and maybe I don't. I certainly don't know all that it is, but that is by the way. But who told you these chaps who want refreshments and ladies' nights and ball games and picnics thought that these things were all of Masonry?"

"No one; but I contend they are not of Masonry. Masonry is grave, dignified, impressive, grand, solemn. Picnics and ball games and entertainments are light and frivolous. They can't possibly mix."

One hundred twenty-six

"Zat so!" commented the Old Tiler. "Go on, you interest me strangely. But before you go on, tell me this: is it irreligious for a church to have a picnic or a social?"

"Why—er—why, no. I suppose not. But it isn't the church that has 'em; it's the Sunday School."

"Yes, where they train little children to be good and to love God and come to church. You would think the minister would know better than to try to impress children with the Fatherhood of God by holding a picnic, wouldn't you? And of course any sort of church entertainment which makes people come and laugh and know each other better and make money to decorate the church is all wrong, wicked, in fact. I should speak to the district attorney about it, if I were you."

"Now you are laughing at me!" protested the New Brother.

"Well, it's more than anyone else will, if you keep up the line of chatter you started with me," went on the Old Tiler. "Listen, Son, till I tell you. Masonry is all you have said it is, and a great deal you haven't said. And religion is a lot more than going to church. But if God can stand to look down and see his ministers and those who love Him and follow Him, having a lot of innocent enjoyment in an entertainment or a ball game or a picnic, I guess it won't hurt Masonry any to do the same thing.

"Masonry is strong as its bonds are strong. Its greatest bond is brotherhood—not charity or relief or knowledge or learning, or ritual, or secrecy—but brotherhood. The feeling you have for the fellow who has sat in lodge with you is brotherhood—you have sworn the same obligations, seen the same work, experienced the same emotions—there is a bond between you. Anything that makes that bond stronger without doing harm in some other way is a help to Masonry.

"A picnic brings you and your brother Mason together informally. It brings your children out together to play together. You find out that Smith is totally different from what he appears in lodge—there he is shy, retiring, almost insignificant. On a picnic he is in his element; playing with the children, having a good time with the men, helping the women—and you like Smith better. There are a thousand Smiths and a thousand of you, and it is a picnic or a ball game or an outing of some sort which brings you together.

"You spoke of ladies' night. Ladies' nights make the ladies happy. They impress women with the idea that Masonry is innocent, happy, a good thing. They find out what sort of men their husbands and brothers and sweethearts and sons see every week or so. They learn to associate a name and a personality with a position; they find out that the Master is human, the Secretary a nice man, the Junior Warden a decent sort, the Senior Warden a delightful fellow. All that makes for the spread of the good repute of the order. Moreover, there are a lot of fellows who don't get so much out of the lodge as they might; its their fault, perhaps, but we are not supposed to go around looking for our brother's faults. If the ladies' night makes the come-but-seldom brother feel that his lodge is doing something for him, it's worth while.

"There are other things to do with money besides hoard it. There are better ways of spending it than to use it upon new costumes and furniture. One of the good ways is to use it to make someone happy. If this lodge has enough spare funds to provide some good eats and drinks for its ladies, then it's a good thing so to spend it. If we have enough cash to finance a picnic or a ball game, it's a good thing to do. And all the gravity and solemnity of the third degree will not be hurt one small iota by all the fun you will have, any more than the reverence we all owe the Creator is in any way damaged by a Sunday School picnic or a church entertainment.

"Don't forget, Son, that Masons are human beings. We do not try to set ourselves off as being better or different or in any way larger, finer or more learned than our fellows. We merely strive towards perfection by means of a fraternal vehicle which the years have proved to be strong, well made, able to carry us to happiness and honor. If it could be damaged by picnics and ladies' night, it would have fallen to pieces long ago. If its dignity was so slight that it was injured by a Masonic ball game, it would have been a laughing stock the day after baseball was invented.

"Son, get outside of Masonry a minute and look in on it: see it for what it is, not for what it merely appears to be during a degree. When you see Masonry as love for one's fellow, brotherhood between men, charity to all, and reverence for God, you won't think that innocent amusements and gambols on the green of life can hurt it."

"Well, I got to go in lodge now," said the New Brother.

"What's your hurry?" asked the Old Tiler.

"Got to go and support the motion to spend enough to give the girls a real feed!" grinned the New Brother, as he retied his apron strings.

On Masonic Wages

"I THINK they ought to revise the ritual. Its got so many things in it that don't seem to apply nowadays———"

"Seems to me I have heard that said about the Bible, too," the Old Tiler answered the Very New Brother. "But go on, tell it to me. What particular part of the ritual do you want changed?"

"Well, take this for instance, 'and pay the craft their wages, if any be due.' Now you know that doesn't mean a thing to-day. We pay 'wages' or dues to the lodge—the lodge doesn't pay us any wages of any kind."

"Is that so? Well, you ought to stick around more and get yours," answered the Old Tiler. "If you haven't been present at a craft payday yet, you sure are out of luck."

"Why, what do you mean? Have I missed anything?"

"I'll say you have. Boy, if you have been a member of the craft for six months and haven't received any Masonic wages, you are evidently among those the fathers of Masonry had in mind when they wrote 'pay the craft their wages if any be due.' You evidently have not had any wages due you, or you would have received them.

"I have been a Mason so long I forget what it's like not to be one. And I get my Masonic wages

One hundred thirty-one

regularly, and always have. I always hope to. I think most members of the Craft get their wages regularly. It's a shame you don't so conduct yourself that some are due you.

"Lemme tell you a few kinds of coin in which my Masonic wages are paid. Last week my son-in-law lost his job through a misunderstanding. He is not a member of the Craft. He came to me to see what I could do. I went down to see his one-time boss. I told him the story as my son-in-law told it to me. The boss looked at me a minute and asked me, 'Is this on the square?' and I told him it was.

"I know you for a true four-square man,' he answered. 'Tell the boy to come back.'

"Last year Brother Michby was in the hospital. Michby is the president of the First National. I went to see him two or three times. I don't think Michby ever had much of an idea about Masonry before he was so ill; he never came much to lodge. Now he never misses a meeting. And he never fails to stop and chat with me going and coming, or when I meet him on the street. He is one of my wages; just a simple little act of brotherhood brought Michby to appreciate that the lodge wasn't just words. I don't know how much good he has done since he has been really interested, but I do know that he lays it all to my visiting him.

"Over the head of my bed is an electric light. I can read before I go to sleep and reach up and turn it off when I am tired. Both it and the books I read came from Brother Tome, who is librarian up at the big temple. Tome heard me trying to explain the meaning of a symbol one time and took me aside and asked me if I had ever read either Mackey or Pike. It sounds foolish now, but then I hadn't and I said never heard of them. The light and the books were the answer. Now I am never without a book of some kind, and it's astonishing what even an Old Tiler can read if he reads long enough. Masonic wages, my boy, Masonic wages are worth much fine gold.

"Two years ago I had some trouble; my little daughter was hurt, you remember or maybe you don't remember. Anyway, she was all smashed up in a street car accident. After I got over the first shock I began to wonder what could be done for the little girl. It looked like a long illness and a hospital, and nurses and doctors and expenses almost beyond my means.

"But I didn't trust the lodge enough. We had seven doctors on the rolls and one of the seven was at the hospital every day. I wasn't ever allowed to see a bill of any sort. Jim, the florist, kept her room a bower. Maxie, the preacher, brought a different young girl to see her every other day, until she had a wonderful circle of friends. Boys I only knew by sight used to stop me on the street or come to the house or the hospital, and when she got well and strong again she always said it was as much because of the loving care everybody took of her father's child as because of the doctors and the surgeons. Masonic wages away beyond my deserts, boy, but Masonic wages nevertheless.

"I am a poor man. I never learned much in the way of a trade or business. I'll never be much of a financial success. But is there a man in this town who knows more men, who can call more big business men by their front names than I can? I used to think maybe it was just because I was Tiler. Now I know it isn't. Men like Michby and Lawyer Repsold and Doctor Cutter and Harrison of the big department store have asked me to their houses to chat Masonry with them, and I've gone just as gladly as I go to the bricklayer and the crossing policeman and the elevator man when they ask me! And when men like these tell me I've meant something in their lives that money can't buy, I don't care a hoot that I never learned much to be paid in cash; I get paid such large Masonic wages that I think the balance is even.

"Oh, no, lad, don't let's revise the ritual. Masonic wages are those which are paid in love and brotherhood and mutual help and information and inspiration and charity and assistance and being pals. They are all worth more, much, much more than mere money. Take the Masonic wages out of a lodge and you would, indeed, need to revise the ritual; you'd need to revise the whole fraternity. The payment Masons make to Masons is the most valuable which a man can receive. And you want to revise it out of existence!"

"No, I don't," answered the New Brother. "Now I'll tell you something. It was Brother Maxie, the preacher, who told me to come and say that to you; he started by telling me how grateful some brother or other was because I had helped him out of a hole, and Maxie asked me if

I'd received any Masonic wages yet. When I told him I hadn't, he said you were paying off and that the way to get paid was to go to you and blatherskite about the ritual and——I've been paid."

"You are a pair of rascals," growled the Old Tiler, but his eyes looked as if he was smiling inside.

LaVergne, TN USA
15 April 2010
179337LV00001B/3/A

9 780766 138940